HARPER CHASE

Nefarious Crimes: Axe Murders

Contents

Introduction

In the annals of criminal history, few weapons strike as deep a chord of primal fear as the axe. A tool designed for the mundane act of chopping wood, when repurposed as an instrument of death, transforms ordinary homes into scenes of nightmarish horror. This narrative delves into the dark corridors of history, shedding light on the most infamous axe murders that have both horrified and fascinated humanity for centuries.

The journey begins in a time before forensic science, where the brutal simplicity of an axe murder left communities grappling with fear and uncertainty. The axe, easily accessible and requiring no special skill to wield, became a symbol of unchecked rage and unspoken terror. Each chapter revisits a different case, unraveling the circumstances, the investigation, the cultural impact, and, where possible, the psychological underpinnings of the killer.

The saga of axe murders is as old as history itself. From the legends of medieval executioners to the grim tales of family annihilators, the axe has been a silent witness to unspeakable acts. Cases span continents and centuries, including the infamous Lizzie Borden case, where the rhyme "Lizzie Borden took an axe..." became a chilling playground chant. The still-unsolved Villisca Axe Murders of 1912, where an entire family was slaughtered in their sleep in a small Iowa town, left a mystery that haunts the community to this day.

Through different eras, the narrative around axe murders shifts with the evolving understanding of criminal psychology. The axe murderers in these pages are not just subjects of macabre curiosity but also prisms through which to view the darker aspects of human nature. What drives an individual to commit such acts of brutality? Is it madness, revenge, a momentary lapse into savagery, or something more insidious and calculated?

This narrative also examines the cultural aftermath of these crimes. The axe murders explored not only shocked the communities in which they occurred but also left an indelible mark on popular culture. They inspired novels, films, and folklore, turning murderers and victims alike into almost mythical figures. In dissecting these stories, it is uncovered how these narratives shaped public perception of crime and justice.

Moreover, it is a testament to the evolution of criminal investigation techniques. Tracing how early investigations, often hampered by lack of scientific methods and reliance on superstition and hearsay, gave way to more sophisticated forensic approaches. These cases, in their brutality and notoriety, often acted as catalysts for change in law enforcement methodologies.

Be prepared to enter a world where the ordinary becomes macabre, where homes become crime scenes, and where the echo of an axe's chop reverberates through history. Each chapter not only tells the story of a particular murder but also offers a window into the era's societal, cultural, and legal landscapes.

It is more than just a compilation of grim tales; it is a thoughtful exploration of a grim chapter in human history, a chapter that offers insights into the complexities of the human psyche, the fragility of societal norms, and the ever-present shadow of violence that looms over civilizations. It is a journey into the heart of darkness, a journey that, while unsettling, is essential for understanding the depths of human depravity and the relentless pursuit of justice.

Written with the utmost respect for the victims and their families, their stories are not just footnotes in history but solemn reminders of lives cut tragically short. As these dark tales are delved into, it is important to remember the human cost of these heinous acts and the enduring impact they have had on communities and history.

Mary Russell Massacre

As dawn broke on June 26, 1828, Cork Harbor in southern Ireland was a hive of activity. Muscular longshoremen effortlessly juggled heavy crates, seagulls danced in the salty air, and an eclectic array of ships bobbed in the shimmering water. To the casual observer, it seemed like just another bustling day at the docks.

Amidst this lively scene, William Scoresby, Jr., a renowned Arctic explorer, scientist, and Anglican minister, was making his way across the harbor. From his vantage point in a small boat, Scoresby absorbed the vibrant harbor life, unaware that his day was about to take a dramatic turn.

As the boat glided through the waters, Scoresby's attention was suddenly captured by a fellow passenger's alarming news: a brutal murder had reportedly occurred aboard a seemingly innocuous brig anchored nearby.

The revelation sent shockwaves through the passengers, sparking a frenzy of curiosity and horror. Disregarding their initial plans, the group, except for one woman, decided to investigate the ghastly rumor. They steered their boat toward the ill-fated brig, where a lone officer on deck chillingly confirmed their worst fears: the crew had indeed been savagely murdered.

Scoresby later recounted in his 1835 memoir "Memorials of the Sea," the harrowing sight that greeted them: five gruesomely mutilated bodies sprawled below the skylight of the cabin, with the remains of two others partially visible.

The officer's bizarre willingness to expose strangers to such a macabre scene was puzzling, but Scoresby's status as a minister might have played a role in gaining their trust, not to mention that his brother-in-law was the first magistrate to arrive at the scene.

This ghastly discovery ignited Scoresby's investigative instincts. Over the following weeks, he painstakingly interrogated survivors, meticulously followed the ensuing trial, and even initiated a years-long correspondence with the murderer himself.

At the heart of Scoresby's investigation lay a haunting question: What could drive a well-regarded, seemingly rational individual to commit such atrocious acts? This query not only fueled his quest for answers but also captivated the public's imagination, marking an unforgettable chapter in Scoresby's storied life.

The brig Mary Russell, a stately vessel, began its fateful journey in the winter of 1827, departing from County Cork to Barbados under the meticulous command of Captain William Stewart. At 53, Stewart was a seasoned mariner, his sharp features and distinctive crop of red hair making him a recognizable figure. The crew's initial task was straightforward: deliver a cargo of mules to the Caribbean. Upon completion, they loaded the brig with an array of goods - sugar, animal hides, and other valuable exports - preparing for the return voyage to Ireland.

However, an unexpected addition to the crew came in the form of Captain James Raynes. Recently relieved of his duties as first mate on another ship due to his burgeoning alcoholism, Raynes found himself in a precarious position. Despite his reservations, Stewart agreed to let Raynes hitch a ride back to Ireland on the Mary Russell, which set sail on May 9, 1828.

The journey's early days were marked by an ominous shift in atmosphere. Stewart, deeply religious and superstitious, experienced a disturbing dream in which Raynes was plotting a mutiny. He interpreted this as a divine warning, a premonition of betrayal. Stewart had reason to suspect Raynes: the disgraced captain was returning to Ireland in shame, his prospects of commanding another vessel dimmed by his reputation as a drunkard. Stewart surmised that Raynes might be desperate enough to attempt piracy, seeing the Mary Russell as a valuable prize ripe for the taking.

Stewart's suspicions deepened as he observed Raynes's interactions with the crew. Raynes frequently shaved in the crew's quarters, a space usually reserved for lower-ranking sailors, and engaged them in conversations in Gaelic, a language unknown to Stewart. This close rapport between Raynes and the crew was unusual and troubling to Stewart. The crew's behavior added fuel to the fire: John Keating inquired about Raynes's navigational skills, while John Howes sought Stewart's guidance in lunar distance, a critical component of celestial navigation.

As the voyage progressed, Stewart's unease grew into full-blown paranoia. He took drastic measures for his safety, enlisting a handful of trusted crew members to sleep in his cabin as a protective measure. He kept an assortment of weapons - an ax, a crowbar, and more - within arm's reach, prepared for any confrontation. In a controversial move, Stewart disposed of essential navigational tools - logbooks, charts, and instruments - overboard, intending to prevent Raynes and any conspirators from commandeering the ship.

The tension aboard the Mary Russell escalated further when Stewart became suspicious of first mate William Smith. Smith's repeated trips to the steerage for oil and materials to repair a lamp were interpreted by Stewart as clandestine activities. Convinced of a brewing mutiny, Stewart demanded that the crew tie up Smith. Initially met with resistance, the crew eventually complied with Stewart's demand, fearing his increasingly unstable behavior. Smith, though reluctant, acquiesced to being confined in a cramped space under the cabin.

This action, however, did little to quell Stewart's mounting anxiety. Convinced that his life was in imminent danger, he began to devise a more extreme plan to ensure his survival.

On the 21st of June, the Mary Russell sailed under a bright, clear sky, her sails billowing majestically as she cut through the waters toward Cork. The crew, proficient in their duties, were taken aback when Captain Stewart ordered them to furl several sails, inexplicably slowing their progress. Though puzzled, they complied without open dissent, a testament to the discipline and respect aboard the vessel.

Except for the captive first mate Smith, sequestered below the cabin, the day on deck was bustling with activity. The ship's apprentices, along with a young boy on a health voyage, were all engaged in various tasks. Periodically, Stewart or one of the apprentices would appear on deck, calling one crew member after another to the cabin for some purportedly urgent task. Curiously, none of these men returned to the deck, and soon, six had vanished into the ship's depths, leaving only two - seaman John Howes and mule tender James Murley - above.

The situation escalated when Howes was summoned. Halfway down the steps, he halted abruptly, confronted by Stewart who was menacingly brandishing pistols. Howes, remarkably composed, questioned Stewart's intentions. The captain, frantic and delusional, accused him of mutiny and demanded his submission. Howes initially fled, dodging Stewart's haphazard gunfire, but then, in a bid to pacify the captain, he and Murley resigned themselves to being bound.

Murley was led to the cabin with the other immobilized sailors, while Howes was restrained on the half-deck. Hours of discomfort led Howes to reconsider his compliance. He managed to loosen his ropes, but Stewart, upon discovering this the next morning, engaged in a violent confrontation. Howes was shot thrice and brutally beaten by the apprentices, whom Stewart had manipulated with a mix of threats and promises of wealth.

In a remarkable turn of events, Howes survived and concealed himself among the cargo crates.

Captain Stewart later confessed to Scoresby that his initial plan was not to harm anyone but to sail the ship alone, seeking rescue from the crew's alleged treachery. He hoped to flag down a passing ship, but his efforts were futile – one ship had already passed during the scuffle with Howes, and another veered away, perhaps mistaking the Mary Russell for a pirate vessel.

Haunted by the missed opportunities for rescue and driven by his own distorted logic, Stewart concluded that if the crew were innocent, God would have ensured their rescue. Thus, he reasoned, their deaths must be divinely ordained as punishment for mutiny. This chilling epiphany, coupled with the fear of Howes potentially emerging from hiding to attack him, led Stewart to a dark and irreversible decision.

Convinced of his divine mandate and tormented by paranoia, Stewart resolved to eliminate his crew.

Captain Stewart, fueled by paranoia and a distorted sense of divine mission, embarked on a horrific spree of violence. Crowbar in hand, he burst into the cabin with a chilling proclamation: "The curse of God is upon you all!" His words barely had time to echo in the cramped space before he unleashed a brutal assault on his helpless crew.

One by one, Stewart viciously bludgeoned his prisoners: second mate William Swanson, James Murley, carpenter John Cramer, seamen Francis Sullivan and John Keating, mule handler Timothy Connell, and James Raynes. Each strike was delivered with a terrifying ferocity. After ensuring they were all incapacitated, Stewart, in a grotesque display of overkill, seized an ax and methodically mutilated each body, ensuring no signs of life remained.

The three young apprentices, mere children aged between 10 and 15, were forced to witness this barbaric act, their faces reflecting sheer terror as blood pooled and streamed through a hole in the cabin floor. Below, first mate William Smith, still confined and immobilized, was subjected to the gruesome spectacle of blood and viscera dripping onto him from above.

Stewart, not yet satisfied, enlarged the hole with his ax and attacked Smith with the crowbar and a harpoon. After checking for a pulse and feeling none, Stewart sat back, his frenzied energy seemingly expended.

In a macabre and chilling moment, Stewart demanded meat and alcohol, consuming them nonchalantly amidst the carnage. He casually smoked his pipe, remarking heartlessly about the bodies as if they were mere animal carcasses. In his mind, he had not only saved his own life but also the Mary Russell and its valuable cargo, rationalizing the massacre as a necessary evil.

When Stewart eventually flagged down the Mary Stubbs, he displayed a shocking lack of remorse. He even bragged about his deeds to Captain Robert Callendar, inquiring if Callendar thought him brave for his actions. The crew of the Mary Stubbs, likely horrified, discovered Howes and Smith. Stewart, upon realizing Smith was alive, expressed a twisted form of remorse, attributing Smith's survival to divine intervention, oblivious to the reality that Smith had narrowly escaped death by shifting his position during the attack.

Howes and Smith were taken aboard the Mary Stubbs for safety. A few of Callendar's men remained on the Mary Russell to assist with navigation. However, Stewart's paranoia quickly resurfaced. He became convinced that these new sailors were plotting against him, leading to two desperate attempts at escaping by throwing himself overboard, only to be rescued each time.

On his transfer to the Mary Stubbs, Stewart's mental state deteriorated further, prompting yet another leap into the sea. This time, he was picked up by a fishing boat, which quickly departed the scene, leaving behind a trail of confusion and horror.

The arrival of the Mary Russell and the Mary Stubbs in Cork Harbor near midnight on June 25th marked the beginning of a legal drama as gripping as the tragic voyage itself. The gruesome tale of the murders aboard the Mary Russell was quickly relayed to the local authorities. A manhunt for the perpetrator, Captain Stewart, was rendered unnecessary as fate had already led him directly into the hands of the Coast Guard. He was taken into custody after candidly recounting his actions in startling detail.

The local jail in County Cork became Stewart's temporary abode, as the coroner swiftly convened a grand jury to deliberate on the charges. The case was complex and confounding. Stewart's murderous rampage seemed entirely at odds with his previous reputation for composure and rationality. There was no concrete evidence suggesting a planned mutiny by his crew. The jury grappled with the possibility of mental illness playing a role in Stewart's actions, a concept that was still murky and poorly understood at the time.

On August 4th, the grand jury indicted Stewart for murder, acknowledging his "state of mental derangement" during the crimes. This nuanced charge laid the groundwork for a trial that would hinge heavily on interpretations of mental illness and criminal responsibility.

The trial, which began a week later, drew crowds of onlookers, all eager to catch a glimpse of the man accused of such heinous acts. Stewart, maintaining an air of respectability in his formal attire, became the center of attention as the prosecutor opened with a statement that delved into the complex interplay between insanity and innocence. The prosecutor clarified that a total inability to discern right from wrong due to mental derangement could lead to a verdict of not guilty by reason of insanity. However, proving this incapacity fell to the defense, while the prosecution focused on establishing the facts of the murder.

The implications of a successful insanity plea were clear: though Stewart might be acquitted, he would not walk free. In line with 19th-century legal practices, he would likely face confinement in an asylum or prison.

The trial unfolded as a tapestry of testimonies and expert opinions, not unlike contemporary trials but steeped in the rudimentary psychiatric understanding of the era. Witnesses recounted the harrowing events aboard the Mary Russell, while medical experts deliberated over Stewart's mental state. A key testimony came from a doctor who suggested Stewart suffered from monomania—a condition where a person could be entirely rational except on one particular subject, which in Stewart's case was an obsessive fear of mutiny.

In his address to the jury, the judge posited that insanity was an affliction ordained by God. He framed the dilemma facing the jury in stark terms: was Stewart's rampage a deliberate act spurred by malevolent forces, or was it the result of a divine intervention that robbed him of his senses? The judge emphasized that if God had indeed stripped a man of his understanding, it fell beyond the purview of any earthly court to punish him. Therefore, in the eyes of the law, being 'guilty' and 'insane' were contradictory states.

However, this nuanced perspective seemed to have been lost in translation to the jury. After an hour and a half of intense deliberation, they returned with a perplexing verdict: Stewart was guilty, yet also insane at the time of the murders. The judge, having just articulated that such a combination was legally untenable, pointed out the contradiction. An assistant judge interposed, clarifying that the verdict effectively amounted to 'not guilty,' as the law did not recognize guilt in the context of insanity. He advised the jury that they could amend their verdict on the spot.

Adjusting their decision, the jury declared Stewart insane and not guilty. Consequently, the judge imposed a sentence of "close confinement during life, or during his Majesty's pleasure," effectively committing Stewart to life imprisonment or until further royal decree.

In a dramatic response, Stewart fell to his knees, clasped his hands in prayer, and expressed a profound sense of relief. He professed gratitude to God, asserting that he had not willfully committed the murders. In his mind, his actions were not borne of malicious intent but were the tragic outcome of a mental condition beyond his control.

This moment in the courtroom encapsulated the complex interplay of law, morality, and mental health in the early 19th century. Stewart's trial and its outcome highlighted the evolving understanding of insanity in the legal system, marking a significant moment in the history of criminal justice and the treatment of mental illness.

The remainder of Captain William Stewart's life unfolded within the confines of various institutions. His journey through the justice system began in Cork's city jail, where he stayed until 1830. He was then transferred to the Cork Lunatic Asylum, remaining there until 1851, before finally being moved to Dundrum Asylum for the Criminally Insane, where he lived until his death at the age of 98 in 1873.

Stewart's long years in confinement were marked by a range of activities and emotional states. He dedicated time to tutoring his children, an act that likely provided a sense of normalcy and connection to the outside world. He also crafted model boats, a nod to his maritime past, which he sold to support his family financially. His commitment to studying the Bible was unwavering, perhaps seeking solace and understanding in its pages.

When William Scoresby, the Arctic explorer and Anglican minister, visited Stewart in August 1829, he found a man resigned to his fate. Stewart expressed no desire for freedom, acutely aware of the social stigma that would follow him. He dreaded being marked forever as the man who had committed such atrocious acts against his crew.

Stewart's mental state fluctuated during his incarceration. He experienced periods of anxiety and depression, and his feelings oscillated between acceptance of his situation and vehement assertions of innocence. This internal turmoil was compounded by his struggle to comprehend his mental illness. However, Stewart found some comfort in his belief that his actions were part of a divine plan, a sentiment echoed by Scoresby and reflective of the prevailing religious mindset of the time.

Scoresby, in his writings, mused on the tragic events, seeing them as a mysterious and dreadful act of divine providence. He called for humility and reverence when speaking of God's might and the inscrutable ways in which it manifests.

In retrospect, Stewart's trial and its aftermath would likely have unfolded quite differently in modern Ireland. The heavily theological lens through which his case was viewed would be replaced by a more secular and clinical approach. Mental illness would be understood in a more nuanced and scientifically informed manner, and Stewart would likely receive more comprehensive psychiatric care and a more precise diagnosis than simply monomania.

Interestingly, despite the advancements in psychiatry and legal frameworks, the fundamental outcome of Stewart's trial might not differ significantly if it were to occur today. Under a 2006 law in Ireland, a verdict of "Not guilty by reason of insanity" remains a viable conclusion for cases where mental illness profoundly impacts the defendant's actions. This continuity highlights the enduring complexity of adjudicating cases at the intersection of criminal law and mental health. Stewart's story, thus, remains a poignant and thought-provoking chapter in the annals of legal and psychiatric history.

Lizzie Borden

Step into the captivating world of Lizzie Andrew Borden, whose life story unfolds like a riveting novel, set against the backdrop of 19th-century Fall River, Massachusetts. Born on a warm summer day, July 19, 1860, Lizzie was the youngest daughter of Andrew Jackson Borden and Sarah Anthony Morse Borden, a couple whose union began on a Christmas Day in 1845. Lizzie's family life was marked by both joy and tragedy: the birth of her beloved sisters, Emma Lenora and Alice Esther, was shadowed by the early demise of Alice before her second birthday, and the heart-wrenching loss of their mother, Sarah, when Lizzie was a mere toddler.

Amidst this early turbulence, a solemn vow was whispered: Emma, barely nine years old, promised their dying mother she would forever be Lizzie's guardian angel.

The Borden household witnessed a new chapter on June 6, 1865, when Andrew remarried, bringing Abigail "Abby" Durfee Gray into their lives. Abby and Andrew's marriage, though childless, offered a semblance of stability. Lizzie and Emma, now bound by an unbreakable sisterly bond, navigated their complex family dynamics into their adult years.

Andrew Jackson Borden, a man of humble beginnings yet ambitious spirit, was the scion of a prominent family that had, by the early 18th century, essentially carved out a significant part of Fall River's landscape as their own. Starting life in a modest setting, Andrew honed his skills as a carpenter, a trade that led him to help construct the very house at 92 Second Street that he would later own. His career trajectory was as diverse as it was impressive: from carpentry to undertaking, where he and business partner William M. Almy found success in the funeral industry, to his eventual ventures into property development and banking.

By the 1850s, Andrew had become a notable figure in Fall River's business circles. His roles ranged from president of the Union Savings Bank to influential positions in several textile mills, including the Globe Yarn Mill Company and the Troy Cotton and Woolen Manufacturing Company. His acumen also led him to directorships at the Durfee Safe Deposit and Trust Co. and the First National Bank, cementing his status as a pillar of the local community.

In April 1872, a new chapter began for the Borden family as they settled into the house at 92 Second Street, a purchase Andrew Borden made for $10,000. This new home became the canvas of their lives, with 21-year-old Emma and 11-year-old Lizzie adapting to their new surroundings.

Andrew Borden, despite his considerable wealth, was a man of stark frugality. His choice to reside in this modest abode, rather than the more upscale neighborhood of "The Hill" where many of his affluent relatives lived, spoke volumes of his simplistic approach to life. This parsimony extended to the very amenities of the house – while he could easily afford modern luxuries like indoor plumbing and electricity, he chose to stick with oil lamps, shunning the extravagance of gas lighting. His thriftiness even led him to sell eggs from his farm on Main Street. Yet, in an intriguing contrast, he didn't shy away from employing servants to maintain their home, a nod to the family's social standing.

This tendency to pinch pennies often led to tensions within the household, particularly with Lizzie, who yearned for the lavish lifestyle of her relatives on "The Hill." The Borden sisters, Lizzie and Emma, maintained a distant relationship with their stepmother, Abby, always addressing her formally as "Mrs. Borden." Their meals were often separate affairs, further highlighting the familial divide.

As Andrew's wealth grew, so did the sisters' concerns about Abby's family potentially eyeing their father's fortune. Despite these undercurrents of unease, the household was deeply rooted in religious faith. The Bordens were regular attendees of the Central Congregational Church, located in the prestigious "Hill" neighborhood. Lizzie, particularly devout, was deeply involved in church activities and even taught Sunday school.

Both Emma and Lizzie, as they matured, began assisting their father in managing his rental properties, taking on roles that reflected their growing responsibilities within the family and the broader community.

Emma Borden, a figure of quiet reserve, was the embodiment of Victorian decorum, seldom venturing beyond the confines of her home. She was seen as the epitome of reliability and propriety. In stark contrast, her younger sister Lizzie was the vibrant flame to Emma's calm ember. With her striking red hair and engaging demeanor, Lizzie was a social butterfly, attracting a number of suitors and companions. Yet, these admirers were not from the elite "Hill" neighborhood, the object of Lizzie's long-held aspirations.

Despite their regular attendance at the church frequented by the town's upper crust, the Bordens remained outsiders within their own community. Andrew's penny-pinching ways and dubious reputation in business circles confined them to a middle-class standing, a stark contrast to their financial capabilities. Lizzie's romantic prospects were further complicated by her father's dismissal of her suitors as mere "fortune hunters," seemingly sealing her and Emma's fate to a life of spinsterhood.

The household's underlying tensions escalated in the months leading up to the infamous murders. A point of contention arose when Andrew gifted real estate to Abby and her sister, prompting Emma and Lizzie to demand a property of their own. They received the house where they had lived until their mother's passing, only to sell it back to their father shortly after for $5,000, a transaction that hinted at the complex family dynamics.

In May 1892, a seemingly trivial incident revealed deeper rifts within the Borden family. Andrew, deeming the pigeons roosting in the barn as nuisances, eradicated them with a hatchet. This act deeply upset Lizzie, who had recently built a roost for these birds. The growing familial discord culminated in July 1892, when a significant argument prompted the sisters to seek solace in an extended "vacation" to New Bedford, Massachusetts. Their return, a week before the tragic events that would mark their lives forever, was staggered. Lizzie chose to stay at a local rooming house for four days before rejoining her family, a decision that would soon be scrutinized under the harsh lens of public and legal scrutiny.

In the days leading up to the grim events of August 4, 1892, an ominous pall hung over the Borden household. The entire family was struck by a mysterious and violent illness. On August 3, amid growing concerns, Abby Borden summoned Dr. Seabury Bowen, fearing they had been poisoned. The doctor, however, attributed their malady to bad food and offered to examine the rest of the family. This suggestion was met with Andrew's ire, who saw the doctor's visit as an unnecessary expense, promptly sending him away.

That same evening, the household's dynamics took another intriguing turn with the unexpected arrival of "Uncle John" Morse, the younger brother of Sarah Morse Borden and the girls' uncle. Although he had been a peripheral figure in Lizzie and Emma's lives, his visits had become more frequent in the two years preceding the murders, often under the guise of familial visits, but with underlying business motives.

His visit on the eve of the murders was allegedly to discuss financial matters with Andrew. This conversation, speculated by some to revolve around property transfers, may have further fueled the already simmering tensions within the household. Morse stayed overnight, occupying an upstairs bedroom, unaware of the horror that the next day would bring.

On the fateful morning of August 4, 1892, the Borden residence became the scene of a ghastly crime. Andrew and Abby Borden were found brutally slain, their lives violently cut short. At this juncture, Lizzie was 32, and Emma 41 – both unmarried and living under their father and stepmother's roof. Notably, Emma was absent on that day, having traveled to Fairhaven, Massachusetts, to visit a friend, about 15 miles from the scene of the crime.

The stillness of the Borden residence was shattered on that fateful day when Lizzie Borden stumbled upon a scene of unimaginable horror. Her father lay lifeless on the sofa, his face unrecognizably disfigured from a brutal bludgeoning. Lizzie's piercing screams echoed through the house, summoning Bridget Sullivan, the maid, who in turn raced to bring Dr. Bowen and a neighbor, Adelaide Churchill, to the ghastly scene.

The horror deepened when Bridget and Adelaide discovered Abby Borden in an upstairs guest room, her head viciously beaten, mirroring the brutality inflicted upon Andrew Borden. The merciless assailant had wielded a small, sharp hatchet with lethal precision, leaving both victims in a state of gruesome demise.

The local police, upon arrival, commenced a frantic search for clues. Their quest for an intruder proved futile, as no evidence suggested an outsider's involvement. In the basement, amidst various tools, they found two hatchets, two axes, and a particularly ominous hatchet head with a freshly broken handle, which they suspected to be the murder weapon. Strangely, no blood was found anywhere except on the bodies of the slain couple.

The crime scene, however, quickly succumbed to chaos, overrun by journalists, neighbors, and other onlookers, leading to significant contamination of crucial evidence. The police, in a display of gross oversight, allowed the family to clean the house, neglecting to thoroughly inspect Lizzie or Bridget for bloodstains or conduct a detailed examination of Lizzie's room. This lax approach would later attract severe criticism for its lack of rigor.

As the investigation unfolded, the authorities narrowed their focus within the Borden home, quickly dismissing Emma, who was away in Fairhaven, and overlooking Bridget Sullivan, the maid. Their suspicions inexorably gravitated towards Lizzie Borden.

Meanwhile, Emma received the grim news of her family's tragedy through a telegram sent by Dr. Bowen, urgently beckoning her back to Fall River.

In a startling development, just two days post-murder, newspapers began circulating reports, rife with speculation and insinuation, hinting at Lizzie Borden's possible involvement in the brutal slaying of her parents. The whispers of suspicion were transforming into a chorus of accusations, marking the beginning of one of the most enigmatic and talked-about murder cases in American history.

The police investigation into the Borden murders unearthed chilling details, painting a timeline of the cold-blooded killings. The first to fall victim was Abby Borden, her body discovered in a state of rigidity, a grim testament to the time that had elapsed since her demise. The coroner's findings were harrowing: Abby had been assaulted sometime between 9 a.m. and 10:30 a.m., her skull mercilessly struck 18 times with a hatchet's brutal force.

The nature of Abby's wounds suggested a face-to-face confrontation with her assailant. The initial blow was delivered to the side of her head, a strike so forceful it caused her to turn and collapse face down. Then, in a relentless onslaught, 17 more blows were rained upon the back of her head, each one a fatal strike in its own right.

At 64 years old, weighing around 200 pounds, Abby was a woman whose character was a topic of varied opinions. To some, she was a dour, affectionless figure; to others, a soul of kindness, generosity, and a desire to please.

In a stark contrast of timing, Andrew Borden's body still retained warmth when discovered, signaling that his murder occurred after Abby's. The coroner estimated his fatal attack between 10:30 a.m. and 11:10 a.m. The ferocity with which Andrew was slain mirrored that of Abby's – he, too, fell victim to a hatchet, his face struck ten times in a gruesome act of violence.

Andrew Borden, at 70 years old, was a figure marked by his distinct appearance – tall and lean, with deep-set dark eyes and a pronounced, stern mouth. The investigation into the tragic events of August 4, 1892, painstakingly pieced together the morning's timeline, revealing the activities of each household member.

The morning unfolded with Andrew Borden and John Morse, the visiting uncle, engaged in conversation in the sitting room. Their exchange lasted nearly an hour before Morse departed around 8:45 a.m., followed by Andrew leaving for his morning walk at about 9:00 a.m.

Meanwhile, the household was a hive of activity: Bridget Sullivan, the maid, busied herself washing windows, Abby Borden tackled the cleaning of the guest room recently vacated by John Morse, and Lizzie Borden was occupied in the dining room with ironing chores.

Andrew's return home at approximately 10:30 a.m. marked the prelude to the discovery of the horrifying scene. It was at around 11:10 a.m. that Lizzie came upon her father's lifeless body.

The gravity of the situation soon enveloped Lizzie herself. She was arrested on August 11, with Andrew Jennings, a long-standing attorney for the Borden family, stepping in to represent her. Lizzie's response to the charges was a firm declaration of her innocence, as she entered a "not guilty" plea. Subsequently, she was transported to the jail in Taunton, Massachusetts, located a mere eight miles north of Fall River.

The ensuing legal proceedings began with a preliminary hearing in Fall River, spanning from August 25 to September 1, 1892. The case then progressed to the grand jury, which deliberated over the evidence from November 7 to 21. The culmination of these hearings led to a pivotal moment on December 2, 1892, when Lizzie Borden was formally indicted for murder.

As the Borden case unraveled, it became a sensational topic for the press, with newspapers across the nation and the world fervently covering every twist and turn. The Boston Daily Globe published stories swirling with rumors of discord between Lizzie and her stepmother Abby, suggesting a deep-seated animosity and a prolonged silence between the two. Yet, in the same breath, these reports were countered by assertions from family members who claimed their relationship was normal.

The Boston Herald painted a more sympathetic picture of Lizzie, emphasizing her impeccable character: "In Lizzie Borden's life there is not one unmaidenly nor a single deliberately unkind act." This perspective stood in stark contrast to the myriad of lurid stories that detailed the murders and speculated wildly on motives and potential culprits.

Amidst this media frenzy, Lizzie found herself confined to a jail cell in Taunton, Massachusetts, awaiting her trial in New Bedford, set to commence on June 5, 1893. By the time the trial was about to begin, Lizzie Borden had transformed into a figure of national intrigue and media sensation.

One of the most startling findings presented at Lizzie's inquest was her attempt to purchase prussic acid, commonly known as cyanide, from a drugstore the day before the murders. This request was denied due to the lack of a prescription. In a controversial turn of events, this potentially damning testimony was suppressed during the trial.

On that fateful morning, a curious scene unfolded: Andrew, returning from his walk around 10:30, found himself locked out, with Bridget Sullivan scrambling to let him in. Amidst this confusion, Bridget claimed to hear Lizzie's laughter echoing down from the upper staircase, a claim Lizzie fervently denied.

The plot thickened when Andrew, stepping back into the house, inquired about Abby. Lizzie's response? A vague story about a note summoning Abby to a sick friend's side - a note, and a friend, that mysteriously never surfaced.

Adding to the intrigue, Lizzie recounted how she had assisted Andrew in swapping his boots for slippers before his nap on the sofa. Yet, in a stark contradiction, the police discovered Andrew's lifeless body still clad in his shoes.

The house itself seemed to conspire in the mystery. With the front door and all first-floor windows securely locked, the only entry point was the kitchen - a place bustling with activity that morning. Could an intruder really have slipped in, committed such heinous acts, and vanished without a trace?

Interrogation only deepened the enigma. Lizzie's responses were a labyrinth of contradictions, her demeanor fluctuating between erratic and eerily composed, a state she attributed to morphine taken for her nerves.

Amidst all this, the most baffling aspect remained - Lizzie, claiming to have been in the barn loft during the murders, a claim contested by the untouched dust and the oppressive heat of the loft that day.

Whispers of missing wills added a sinister undertone. Rumor had it that Andrew's will favored his wife, potentially leaving his daughters with little. But, if Abby had perished first, the inheritance would default to his daughters.

Lizzie's defense team, spearheaded by her attorney, painted a picture of a devoted daughter, deeply entrenched in her church, charity work, and community service. They aimed to portray her as someone incapable of the heinous acts she was accused of. On the other side, Prosecutor Hosea Knowlton portrayed a narrative steeped in familial animosity, emphasizing the sheer brutality of the crimes and Lizzie's alleged disdain for her stepmother, Abby.

In a poignant show of sisterly solidarity, Emma Borden stood unwaveringly by Lizzie, taking the stand to vouch for her character and innocence.

Yet, in a strategic move, Lizzie herself remained silent, never taking the stand, her inquest testimony conspicuously absent from the trial's evidence.

Then came the moment of reckoning: On June 20, 1893, after a mere 90 minutes of deliberation, the jury returned with a verdict that would echo through history - Lizzie Borden, acquitted of all charges. The absence of concrete forensic evidence to tie her to the crime scene played a pivotal role. The courtroom erupted as Lizzie released a yelp of elation upon hearing the verdict, a sound that resonated with both relief and disbelief.

The media's reaction was as varied as the opinions of the public. The New York Times, in a post-verdict analysis, expressed a sentiment of relief and approval, noting the jury's swift decision as a telling sign of Lizzie's perceived innocence.

Yet, the story did not end there. The mystery only deepened, as no other suspects were pursued, leaving the case eternally unsolved and shrouded in speculation.

The public and historians alike have since spun numerous theories about how Lizzie managed to escape conviction. Was it her demure, Christian demeanor that swayed opinions, or perhaps her petite stature that led many to underestimate her? Or was it a societal reluctance to condemn a woman to a fate as grim as execution?

After her acquittal, Lizzie Borden, now cloaked in the shadow of notoriety, returned to the familiar walls of her family home, her sister Emma by her side. Yet, the acquittal did little to quell the whispers and wary glances of her townsfolk in Fall River, Massachusetts. In the court of public opinion, Lizzie remained a figure of intrigue and suspicion, a woman acquitted in law but not in the eyes of her community.

Despite the cold shoulder from her neighbors, Lizzie stood her ground, choosing to remain in the town that had turned its back on her.

Andrew Borden's demise left behind a substantial fortune. At 70, he had amassed an impressive portfolio of properties and investments in local mills, leaving an estate valued at a staggering $300,000 - a fortune by today's standards, translating to over eight million dollars. The settlement of his estate, which included payments to Abby's family, eventually funneled a significant portion of this wealth into the hands of Lizzie and Emma.

With this newfound financial freedom, Lizzie's long-held aspiration materialized. She purchased a grand residence, a Queen Anne Victorian mansion she christened "Maplecroft." This luxurious abode, boasting eight bedrooms, four bathrooms, and six fireplaces sprawled over 4,000 square feet, was a testament to her wealth and status. Here, in this lavish setting, Lizzie, now going by the name Lizbeth, employed live-in maids, a housekeeper, and a coachman, surrounding herself with the trappings of affluence.

Yet, despite her attempts to assimilate into the elite circles of her new affluent neighborhood, the specter of her past clung to her. Lizzie continued to attend her church, seeking acceptance within the upper echelons of society she had longed to join. However, the barrier of her infamous legacy proved insurmountable. Former friends and acquaintances distanced themselves, replacing warm greetings with cold shoulders and averted gazes. Lizzie's dream of societal acceptance remained just beyond her grasp, overshadowed by the enduring whispers and sidelong glances of a community that could not forget the shadows of her past.

In the aftermath of her trial, Lizzie Borden's actions only fueled the flames of public scrutiny and disdain. Defying conventional expectations, she shunned the traditional mourning attire, choosing instead to parade her newfound wealth. Lizzie's life became a public spectacle of extravagance and defiance. She lavished herself with a splendid carriage drawn by two magnificent horses, adorned herself in the latest fashion, and embarked on lavish trips to Boston, New York, and Washington D.C., where she indulged in her passion for theater from the comfort of the most luxurious hotels.

The press, ever hungry for sensational stories, latched onto her opulent lifestyle. The Fall River Globe, in particular, seemed to have a vendetta against her, marking the anniversary of the gruesome murders each year with an article that unapologetically cast suspicion on Lizzie.

As the whispers and rumors grew, so did the hostility of those around her. Her once-familiar home became the target of vandalism, with eggs hurled against its walls. The sanctity of church services was marred by the cold shoulder of fellow congregants. Even the innocent pastime of children was tinged with dark undertones, as they chanted a chilling rhyme that echoed the accusations against her: "Lizzie Borden took an axe and gave her mother 40 whacks. When she saw what she had done, she gave her father 41."

Lizzie's already tarnished reputation suffered another blow in 1897, when she found herself embroiled in a scandalous accusation of shoplifting in Providence, Rhode Island. This incident only added more grist to the mill of public opinion, painting her as a figure mired in controversy and suspicion.

In the serene setting of Fall River's upscale neighborhood, the Borden sisters' lives took a dramatic turn in 1904 with the arrival of Nance O'Neill, an actress who quickly formed a close, and somewhat controversial, bond with Lizzie. Rumors swirled about the nature of their relationship, with some speculating a romantic connection. Emma, ever the guardian of propriety, viewed this friendship with disapproval. The final straw came in 1905 when Lizzie hosted a lavish party for O'Neill and her theatrical entourage at their home. In a move that shocked the local community, Emma abruptly left the household.

Emma's whereabouts immediately after her departure remained shrouded in mystery, but by 1923, she was found residing in a nursing home in Newmarket, New Hampshire. Her relocation was partly due to health reasons and perhaps an attempt to escape the persistent shadow of the Borden legacy, especially following the release of yet another book about the infamous murders.

Meanwhile, Lizzie, ever the socialite, continued her life in the grandeur of Fall River. Swapping her horse-drawn carriage for a luxurious limousine, she remained a figure of fascination, continuing her travels even as she aged into a stout, matronly figure.

Tragedy struck again in 1926 when Lizzie underwent gallbladder surgery, leading to a period of chronic illness. She succumbed to pneumonia on June 1, 1927, in her beloved Fall River. Her funeral was a quiet affair, with few attendees, a stark contrast to the life she once led. Emma passed away just nine days later on June 10, 1927, in Newmarket, from kidney complications.

The sisters were laid to rest beside their father in the family plot at Oak Grove Cemetery, their lives forever entwined in history.

Today, the Borden legacy lives on. The infamous murder house at 92 Second Street, now 230 Second Street, stands as a Bed and Breakfast Inn and museum, drawing curious visitors from around the world. Lizzie's "new" house in the Highland District, once a symbol of her liberation and controversy, remains a private residence, a silent witness to the enduring mystery of the Borden story.

Murder of Helen Jewett

On a brisk and unexpected cold night on April 9, 1836, New York City found itself shivering at the tail end of what was the longest and coldest winter of the early 19th century. After a fierce storm had blanketed the northeast in snow just days before, a thaw was beginning to hint at the long-awaited arrival of spring. The Hudson River, which had been a frozen highway since mid-December, saw its first steamboats since the onset of winter bravely slicing through the ice from Albany to Manhattan.

In the heart of downtown Manhattan, just blocks from the bustling streets of Broadway, Rosina Townsend, the astute proprietress of a well-regarded brothel on Thomas Street, was jolted awake in the early hours of April 10. A man's knock at her door broke the night's stillness, seeking exit from the locked house. Her response, sharp yet from her bed, was a reminder of the house rule: "Get your woman to let you out." It was a well-known rule among her nine young residents that the door was locked at midnight, requiring a key from both sides—a measure to prevent mischief and theft. Yet, unusually, no one came to claim the key.

A short while later, a loud knocking stirred Rosina again, this time from the street door. It was a regular client, arriving late for an appointment with Elizabeth Salters, one of the residents. Stealthily confirming his identity, Rosina let him in, only to discover an unsettling clue—a lamp, distinct in its design, glowing unusually in the parlor. This discovery led her to a slightly open backyard door, a security breach in a space she had fortified after previous incidents of unwelcome intrusion. This garden, a secluded oasis amidst the urban sprawl, was now a silent witness to the night's unfolding mystery.

In the eerie silence of the early morning, with a chill still hanging in the air, Rosina Townsend felt a growing unease. The back door of her establishment on Thomas Street was inexplicably open, an unusual occurrence considering the cold weather and the indoor conveniences provided for her guests. She ventured out, her voice echoing into the darkness as she called out, seeking an answer to the unsettling quiet. Finding no response, she secured the door and embarked on a mission to discover the source of the anomaly.

Ascending the stairs with a sense of foreboding, Rosina navigated the dimly lit hallway of her brothel, now a labyrinth of secrets and shadows. She checked the rooms, first Maria Stevens' where all was as expected, and then Helen Jewett's, where she was met with a door ajar and a room engulfed in smoke. Panic surged through her as she envisioned Helen and her guest, potentially suffocating within. Her alarm spread like wildfire, rousing the house with cries of "Fire!"

Chaos ensued as Rosina, her voice piercing the night, alerted the street of the danger. Watchmen, guardians of the city's peace, converged from nearby posts, their presence a small comfort in the unfolding terror. Amidst the smoke and confusion, Rosina and Maria Stevens made a valiant attempt to rescue Helen and her companion, only to be met with a scene that chilled their souls. There, amidst the smoldering remains of the bed, lay Helen Jewett, her life extinguished in the most horrific of ways. Her body bore the gruesome marks of violence, a stark contrast to the peaceful slumber she should have been in. The man who had been her guest, a shadow in the night's events, was conspicuously absent. In this house of secrets and whispers, a brutal murder had unfolded, leaving more questions than answers in its smoky wake.

News of the ghastly discovery at her house traveled rapidly across the country, propelled by the era's burgeoning network of newspapers. Rosina, a woman previously known only within certain circles in Manhattan, was thrust into a glaring public spotlight, her name becoming synonymous with a sensational crime that would echo in public consciousness for years.

In the days following the tragic event, Rosina's recounting of that fateful night became a narrative she was compelled to repeat. Her story, a vivid and melodramatic portrayal of the discovery of Helen Jewett's body, was recorded by journalists and court scribes alike. Despite minor discrepancies, her testimony remained remarkably consistent across various retellings. But as the trial of Jewett's alleged murderer unfolded, Rosina's narrative transformed from a mere recounting of events to a pivotal piece of evidence. She stood as the prosecution's star witness, her credibility under relentless scrutiny by defense attorneys who sought to tarnish her reputation and suggest her own involvement in the crime.

Meanwhile, the immediate aftermath of Rosina's cry for help brought a flurry of activity to her establishment. Four watchmen arrived, initially mistaking the chaos for a mere scuffle. As they realized the gravity of the situation, they, along with some of the women, frantically worked to extinguish the fire in Helen's room. Amidst the pandemonium, a handkerchief marked with a man's name was discovered and seized as potential evidence. The atmosphere was thick with tension and fear; the overnight guests, in various states of disarray, hastily disappeared into the night as soon as the opportunity arose. In this frenzied escape, a woman from the third floor also vanished, her departure hinting at a hasty and indefinite leave.

In the pre-dawn hours of a 1836 New York City, a crime scene was unfolding, one that would soon engage the modest but crucial forces of law enforcement of the era. The city's watchmen, primarily laboring men seeking additional income, were the frontline of a rudimentary security system, their main tasks being to watch for fires and deter common crimes. This network, lacking a formal police force, was bolstered by a handful of full-time police and watch officers, among whom were George Noble, the assistant captain of the watch, and Dennis Brink, a seasoned constable of the Fifth Ward.

As news of the murder at 41 Thomas Street rippled through the city, Noble and Brink, along with other watchmen, converged on the scene. Their arrival marked the beginning of a meticulous investigation in the dim light of early morning. Their first hypothesis led them to the backyard, where they believed the perpetrator may have made an escape. This theory gained traction with the discovery of a hatchet and a long cloak near the fence, suggesting a hurried departure over the barricades and into the labyrinth of the city's back alleys.

In their quest for answers, Brink and Noble interrogated the residents of the brothel, weaving together the narrative of the preceding night. Rosina Townsend, the mistress of the house, recounted the events, identifying the victim as Helen Jewett, a young woman whose name seemed to interchange with 'Ellen' in the confusing mix of identities common in the city's underbelly. She detailed Helen's visitors from the previous evening, notably excluding a regular named Bill Easy at Helen's request and admitting a man known as Frank Rivers. Rivers, who had taken measures to conceal his identity, spent the night in Helen's company, his departure unnoted.

The investigation narrowed its focus on Frank Rivers, who was last seen lounging in Helen's bed. A tip led the policemen to his business address and subsequently to his real identity: Richard P. Robinson, a young clerk residing not far from the scene of the crime. As dawn broke over New York, the pieces of a complex puzzle were slowly falling into place, with the city's rudimentary yet determined law enforcement on the trail of a suspect who was about to become central to one of the most talked-about cases of the time.

Nestled near Greenwich Street stood the boardinghouse of Mrs. Rodman Moulton on Dey Street. This dwelling, bustling with the energy of young men seeking their fortunes in New York, was known colloquially as Mrs. Moulton's house. Reflecting societal norms, it was considered a woman's duty to manage such domestic establishments. Cramped and lively, the house was a stark contrast to the more spacious Thomas Street residence, with its many bedrooms often hosting two or three boarders each.

This boardinghouse was a microcosm of youthful ambition. Its residents, hailing from rural New England and upstate New York, represented the aspiring middle and upper classes. These young men, freed from the constraints of farm life, came to New York with dreams of careers in commerce and the professions, far beyond the horizons of their hometowns. Among them was Richard Robinson, whose family background in Connecticut was marked by landownership and political prominence. George P. Marston, known as Bill Easy, was another such youth, the son of a legal luminary in Massachusetts. These young men embodied the spirit of the era, seeking to master the intricacies of business in the bustling mercantile environment of New York.

A decade or two earlier, these young aspirants would have been apprenticed, living under the roofs and strict supervision of their employers in a quasi-familial setup. But as the 1820s and 1830s unfolded, the dynamics of urban life shifted. The rise of omnibuses and the expansion of residential districts allowed merchants to separate their homes from their workplaces. This change left young clerks like Robinson and Marston to navigate city life independently, living in boardinghouses or above their workplaces. This new arrangement birthed a unique masculine youth culture, largely unsupervised and self-directed. Efforts by merchants to provide some guidance, like the Apprentice's Library with its moralistic literature and lectures, were well-intentioned but often inadequate in the face of the city's myriad temptations.

At the Moulton's, the atmosphere was markedly different from the traditional, supervised apprenticeship model. There was no semblance of family life or oversight; the boarders were left to their own devices, often dining at oyster bars and cafes according to their whims. Each resident had his own key, symbolizing their independence. Richard Robinson shared his room with James Tew, another young man on a similar journey, symbolizing the collective quest of these ambitious youths to carve out their destinies in the vibrant, unforgiving landscape of New York City.

In the early hours of a Sunday morning, the quiet of Mrs. Moulton's boardinghouse was disrupted by the arrival of Officers Noble and Brink. Greeted by a servant girl, a necessity in the bustling environment of a boardinghouse teeming with young men, they swiftly made their way to the room shared by Richard Robinson and James Tew. The scene that unfolded there was a blend of urgency and routine: Tew, roused from sleep, woke Robinson, who seemed deeply asleep until the moment he was informed of the policemen's presence.

As Robinson dressed, hastily pulling on his trousers, a detail caught Brink's eye: a whitewash or paint stain on one of the pant legs. The policemen's request was simple yet ominous – they wanted Robinson to accompany them to the Police Office, with Tew volunteering to join in a show of camaraderie. Amidst this, a question about a dark cloth cloak was raised, to which Robinson confidently replied that he owned none such, only a camblet cloak, a garment of wool and silk luxury.

The calm demeanor Robinson maintained during this encounter struck both Noble and Brink as peculiar. Even as the carriage deviated from its expected route to the Police Office, veering towards the brothel on Thomas Street, Robinson's composure barely wavered. It was only upon learning of Helen Jewett's death and his subsequent arrest for her murder that he showed a flicker of emotion, vehemently denying the charge.

The scene at the Thomas Street house was a tableau of tension and anticipation. The parlor was crowded with the remaining women residents, watchmen, the city coroner, and the city's highest-ranking police magistrate. The arrival of neighboring brothel keepers, Mary Berry and Mary Gallagher, added to the charged atmosphere. Gallagher's interaction with Robinson was particularly poignant. Her direct accusation met with his vehement denial, a protestation of innocence underpinned by a claim to a bright future and the presence of another man's marked handkerchief at the crime scene.

Robinson's request to see the body, a request denied by the police, was interrupted by Brink's caution to Mrs. Gallagher. The moment underscored the delicate balance of investigation and rights, a dance of questions and silences in the face of a heinous crime.

The grim ritual of confronting a murder suspect with the victim's body, a haunting vestige of early American criminal legal practices, was not spared for Richard Robinson. In the past, such a moment was steeped in superstition, where a bleeding corpse at the touch of the suspect was seen as divine intervention, a clear indication of guilt. By the 1830s, this ritual had evolved in New York: now, the focus was on the suspect's reaction rather than any supernatural occurrence. Robinson, maintaining his innocence, was led to Jewett's room to face the harrowing sight of her bloody and charred remains. The officers observing him were struck by his unflinching composure, a stark contrast to the brutality of the scene before him.

The investigation progressed with the arrival of Dr. David L. Rogers and Dr. James B. Kassam, tasked with performing an autopsy. Rogers, a surgeon renowned for his expertise and daring in performing risky operations like ovariotomies, joined Kassam in a meticulous examination of Jewett's body. Their findings painted a grim picture: wounds on the forehead lethal enough to cause instant death, a body unmarred by struggle, and evidence suggesting that the horrifying burns were inflicted postmortem.

The process of legal inquiry continued with the formation of a coroner's jury, hastily assembled from bystanders. In a scene reminiscent of impromptu civic duty, these twelve men were charged with hearing the testimonies of various witnesses gathered at the brothel. Rosina Townsend recounted under oath the events leading up to the discovery of Jewett's body, while others like Elizabeth Salters and Emma French corroborated seeing Robinson at the house on the fateful night. Mary Berry, a neighboring brothel keeper, identified Robinson as a regular visitor known as Frank Rivers. The discovery of the hatchet and cloak by watchmen, along with the details of Robinson's arrest, were also laid bare before the jury. Dr. Rogers' autopsy report added a clinical yet chilling dimension to the proceedings, outlining the physical realities of Jewett's untimely death.

In the midst of the investigation, James Tew, Richard Robinson's roommate, found himself entangled in a situation far beyond his expectations. His presence at the crime scene, initially voluntary in support of Robinson, had become obligatory under the watchful eye of Coroner Schureman. Tew's testimony, crucial yet fraught with ambiguity, painted a picture of the previous evening that was notably vague and inconsistent. He recounted spending time with Robinson until their paths diverged near the American Museum. His own visit to the Thomas Street house, where he briefly conversed with Elizabeth Salters, was reluctantly admitted, given Salters' presence at the inquest.

Throughout the trial, Tew steadfastly maintained his account of Robinson's whereabouts, despite not verifying the times against any clock. This lack of precise timing paradoxically lent a veneer of credibility to his narrative, as a dishonest witness might have been more exact. However, Tew's credibility wavered under the weight of his claims about Robinson's acquaintance with Helen, contradicting the knowledge of several women at the brothel. His hesitant recognition of the cloak found near the crime scene, coupled with his visible agitation, further implicated Robinson in the murder.

The coroner's jury, having deliberated over the amassed testimonies and evidence, concluded that Helen Jewett's death was a result of a hatchet attack by Richard P. Robinson. This verdict led to Robinson's transfer to Bridewell, a decrepit jail with a history of housing American soldiers during the Revolutionary War. Now serving as a debtors' prison and holding cell,

Bridewell became the site of public fascination, with reporters gathering to glimpse the unflustered Robinson, his last request being for cigars to smoke in his cell.

As the official proceedings wound down, the brothel remained a hub of morbid curiosity. Rosina Townsend, seizing the moment, narrated her experience to an audience of young men in the parlor. Outside, a line of onlookers, including neighborhood porter William Van Ness, formed to view Jewett's body, a grim attraction overseen by watch officers. The day's sensational events drew to a close with the admission of James Gordon Bennett, editor of the New York Herald, for a private tour of the crime scene, his journalistic duty granting him access past the throng of spectators.

James Gordon Bennett, the forty-one-year-old Scottish editor of the New York Herald, stood out among the city's newspapermen for his enterprising spirit and flair for sensational reporting. On his visit to the crime scene, he conveyed a sense of self-importance as he navigated through the crowd and past the guard, entering the world of Rosina Townsend's brothel. Bennett's description of the parlor, with its luxurious furnishings, mirrors, and opulent decor, set the stage for his readers, painting a vivid picture of this den of vice and luxury.

Ascending to the second floor, Bennett's narration transformed the gruesome scene into a macabre tableau for his readers. The sight of Helen Jewett's charred and mutilated body, lying on the floor beneath a linen sheet, struck him with an eerie sense of beauty amidst the horror. He compared her corpse to a marble statue, noting the paradoxical blend of violence and grace in her appearance. The bloody gashes on her brow and her burned skin, likened to bronzed sculpture, were detailed with a blend of fascination and revulsion.

His, however, tactically omitted the stark realities of the autopsy. He chose to ignore the disfiguring incisions that had been made during the examination, focusing instead on preserving a romanticized image of Jewett's body. His narrative favored a sexualized, idealized depiction of the corpse over the harsh truth of its post-mortem state, portraying Jewett as an artistic creation marred by violence rather than a victim of a brutal dissection.

Exploration of Jewett's room revealed a space that defied the conventional expectations of a brothel bedroom. He noted her "small library" containing works by notable authors like Lord Byron and Sir Walter Scott, recent literary periodicals, and an array of theatrical sketches. The presence of these items, along with a worktable scattered with writing materials and an album of copied poems, painted Jewett as a woman of intellect and taste. This discovery was further underscored by the trove of letters found in her trunk, seized by the police as potential evidence.

The portrayal of Jewett in his report blended the tragic with the poetic, casting her as a woman of beauty and intellect, tragically cut down in her prime. His narrative, while omitting the harsher aspects of the crime scene, offered his readers a glimpse into a life that was as complex as it was tragic, culminating in a "remarkable end" for a "remarkable character."

He returned to the brothel at 41 Thomas Street on April 12, accompanied by a young lawyer named William Wilder. Their mission: to delve deeper into the mysterious murder of Helen Jewett. Bennett's skepticism about Richard P. Robinson's guilt was growing, and he couldn't help but question if a young man of Robinson's standing could be capable of such brutality. He pondered aloud in his article, suggesting that perhaps a woman, driven by desperation or jealousy, could be the true perpetrator. This angle played into societal prejudices, contrasting Robinson's respectable background with the assumed moral decay of the brothel's inhabitants.

Inside, Rosina Townsend was a whirlwind of conversation, endlessly re-counting the night of the murder. Meanwhile, Bennett explored the house, uncovering further layers of Helen's world. Her room, now a disarray from the police investigation, revealed books like Lalla Rookh, Don Juan, and Beppo, hinting at Helen's romantic and literary inclinations. Bennett even found Lady Blessington's "Flowers of Loveliness," untouched by the fire, adding another layer to Helen's complex personality. These literary tastes, Bennett mused, painted a portrait of a woman drawn to tales of love and adventure, transcending class barriers.

Downstairs, Bennett's attention was caught by a painting of a white woman menaced by tomahawk-wielding Indigenous men. He speculated wildly that such imagery could have influenced the psyche of someone in the house, hinting at violence and jealousy. Bennett's articles were turning the murder into a saga of intrigue and suspicion, far beyond the scope of a simple crime.

April 10, the day of the murder, had begun with the promise of spring, but by nightfall, the city was engulfed in a storm of speculation and scandal. Robinson, confined to jail yet seemingly unfazed, was just one piece of a larger puzzle. Rosina Townsend, reveling in her unexpected fame, provided endless fodder for the press. And the newspapers, led by Bennett's Herald, were in a frenzy to uncover every salacious detail of Helen's life and the circumstances of her death.

The questions swirling around the case – the identity of the murderer, the motive, the potential involvement of other suspects – mirrored the uncertain end of winter in New York. And just as the city thought spring was finally arriving, a fresh blanket of snow on April 13 served as a stark reminder that nothing was as it seemed. The murder mystery, like the delayed spring, lingered, casting a long shadow over the city.

John Lynch the Berrima Axe Murderer

Born into the rolling green hills of Cavan, Ireland, around 1812, John Lynch's tale begins as the son of Owen Lynch. The Lynch family's life took a dramatic turn when John's older brother, Patrick, was embroiled in a scandalous sheep-stealing case in July 1831. Convicted at the Cavan courts, Patrick faced a harsh verdict: transportation for life. He was shipped off to Sydney on the Captain Cook, a journey that began his new life in April 1832.

Meanwhile, John and his father Owen found themselves caught in their own web of legal troubles. In October 1831, both stood before the stern judges in Cavan. Young John, merely 19, was accused of deceitfully obtaining goods, a crime that earned him a life sentence. Owen, at 55 and a widower, faced charges of possessing stolen goods, leading to seven years of transportation. Together, they embarked on a perilous voyage aboard the Dunvegan Castle. Leaving Dublin on 1 July 1832, they faced the unknown, arriving in Sydney on 16 October.

In this new world, John, known for his skills as a ploughman, was assigned to James Atkinson at Oldbury Farm in the Bong Bong district near Berrima. Owen's fate led him to Richard Brownlow, a Sydney publican. Tragedy struck again when Owen passed away on 26 February 1834 in the Gaol Hospital at Sydney, closing his chapter at about 58 years.

In the early days of 1836, Oldbury Farm's overseer, George Barton, encountered a harrowing ordeal on a quiet district road. Ambushed by what were believed to be ruthless bushrangers, he was robbed, bound to a fence, and mercilessly whipped. Suspicions pointed towards a notorious gang led by the infamous John Wales, alias Watt. This gang was a scourge in the area, instilling fear and chaos.

The law soon caught up with Watt and his accomplice, Timothy Pickering, in a dramatic shoot-out along the Cowpasture River. In this fierce encounter, another gang member, John Carpenter, met his end. Watt and Pickering were swiftly tried for an earlier armed robbery and condemned to the gallows, their execution carried out just eight days later.

Meanwhile, George Barton's life took a pivotal turn. In February 1836, he transitioned from overseer to master of Oldbury Farm, following his marriage to Charlotte Atkinson, the widow of James Atkinson.

Amidst these turbulent times, on 12 August 1836, a grim discovery unfolded at Oldbury Farm. Thomas Smith, another convict assigned to Barton, was found murdered, his body hidden in a fallen tree's hollow, a mile from the convict huts. Nearby lay two bloodied pieces of wood, hinting at a violent end. Smith had recently been embroiled in a minor controversy over a lost saddle and bridle but was released from the local watch-house, only to be found dead days later.

The murder investigation zeroed in on John Lynch and John Williamson, two of Barton's convicts. The case hinged on the shaky testimony of Michael Hoy, who shared a hut with the accused and the victim. Hoy suggested that Lynch and Williamson harbored a grudge against Smith, suspecting him of implicating Lynch in the earlier assault on Barton. However, Hoy's credibility was questioned, especially when Barton, in a state of inebriation, failed to provide coherent testimony, earning himself a fine for his courtroom conduct.

In the absence of solid evidence and given Hoy's dubious character, the jury acquitted Lynch and Williamson. However, in a shocking twist, Lynch confessed to the murder a mere day before his scheduled execution six years later.

The saga didn't end there. With other charges looming, Lynch and Williamson were remanded for further proceedings, their fates uncertain in the hands of the law. The Attorney General proposed sending them to Bong Bong magistrates for summary judgment on separate misconduct charges.

The Berrima correspondent for the Sydney Herald, reflecting on Lynch's arrest in February 1842, succinctly captured this period: "He has been a long time in irons in different parts, and he is now a runaway." Lynch's journey through these years was marked by hardship and deceit, particularly during his time in a convict stockade gang in Newcastle.

In a dramatic turn of events on the night of 27 June 1839 in Newcastle, Lynch emerged with a stab wound, claiming he was victimized by fellow inmates Thomas Barry, Thomas Bolson, and Charles Wilson. His tale was one of betrayal and clandestine activities: he accused the trio of retaliating against him for exposing their illicit trade of bartered straw hats for extra rations. According to Lynch, he was asleep when they ambushed him, smothered his face with a blanket, and proceeded to stab him.

The accused men faced the stern justice of the Supreme Court in Sydney in August 1839, where they were initially sentenced to death. However, their sentences were later commuted to transportation to a penal settlement in September of the same year. In a shocking revelation made just before his execution in April 1842, Lynch confessed that the entire episode was a fabrication. The wounds were self-inflicted, a dark plot to exact revenge on the men, resulting in their wrongful transportation.

Lynch also made a startling claim in his confession about his sentence. He asserted that the "life" sentence documented in the convict indents was a clerical error, and that he was actually sentenced to only seven years. He recounted how, after serving his supposed term, he sought freedom at Hyde Park Barracks but left in frustration without a clear answer, eventually making his way back to the Berrima district, where he had previously been assigned.

Despite his claim, it's more likely that Lynch's return to Berrima was the result of him absconding from captivity, adding another layer of intrigue and deception to his already complex and dark history.

In July 1841, John Lynch made a shadowy return to the Berrima district, setting in motion a series of sinister events. His first stop was John Mulligan's farm at Wombat Brush, a place tangled in his past crimes. Mulligan, an emancipated convict and former accomplice in Lynch's robberies, was less than eager to part with the proceeds of their previous escapades, leaving Lynch empty-handed.

Undeterred, Lynch stealthily visited the Oldbury Estate, once his assigned workplace, now under Thomas Humphrey's ownership. There, he brazenly stole eight bullocks from a paddock, plotting to sell them in Sydney. As he drove the bullocks toward the city, fate brought him to Edmund Ireland, a ticket-of-leave holder, and his Aboriginal assistant, both managing a dray loaded with produce.

In a chilling turn, Lynch, harboring a dark plan, brutally murdered both Ireland and the boy with a tomahawk, disposing of their bodies in a secluded rocky cleft. After the cold-blooded act, he lingered at the Razorback campsite, joined by two other teams led by Lee and Leggs, before continuing towards Sydney.

On Dog Trap Road, near Parramatta, Lynch parted ways with the other carriers. He soon encountered Thomas Cowper, the dray's owner, spinning a tale of a broken leg and a hospital visit to explain the absence of his driver and the boy. Cowper, unsuspecting, headed to Sydney, while Lynch, desperate to sell his stolen goods, pushed the team through the night to reach the city ahead of schedule.

Upon arriving in Sydney, Lynch's cunning continued. He enlisted a half-intoxicated man to help sell the pilfered items, perpetuating his web of deceit and crime, a testament to his dark and manipulative nature.

John Lynch's descent into infamy continued as he ventured back towards Berrima with Cowper's dray and team, a stolen convoy under his command. His journey took a fateful turn near Razorback when he encountered a horse team owned by Samuel Bawtree and driven by William Fraser and his son, a young man of about 20. Deciding to join their company, they set up camp for the night at Bargo Brush, where they were later joined by a small group traveling in a cart.

Under the cover of night, as Lynch lay hidden beneath the dray and the others slept by the fire, a police constable arrived on horseback, inquiring about Cowper's missing dray. Lynch, overhearing the conversation and trembling with fear, listened as the Frasers unknowingly protected him by claiming no knowledge of such a dray. The constable's visit stirred a sinister plan in Lynch's mind: to eliminate the Frasers and seize their dray.

Claiming to search for his bullocks the next morning, Lynch instead drove them into the bush. Convincing the Frasers that his team was likely heading back to Berrima, he stashed Cowper's dray and transferred his belongings onto the Frasers' vehicle, continuing along the road with them.

Their journey paused at Cordeaux's Flat, close to Berrima. The next morning, 16 August 1841, Lynch joined the younger Fraser in a search for horses. Concealing a tomahawk within his coat, he waited for the right moment and struck the young man down with a single, lethal blow. He returned to camp alone, deceiving the elder Fraser with a tale of his son still searching for horses. Seizing another opportunity, Lynch delivered a fatal blow to the unsuspecting father, dragging his body into the bush where he buried both father and son.

With his grim task completed late in the day, Lynch spent another night at Cordeaux's Flat, a murderer concealed by the darkness, his conscience as shadowed as the night around him.

In the latter half of 1841, John Lynch's trail of terror weaved through the Berrima district to an appalling climax. Arriving at John Mulligan's farm at Wombat Brush with a stolen horse team, he found Mulligan, an old accomplice, living with his de facto wife, Bridget Macnamara, and her two children, John and Mary. Lynch, seeking a payout from past crimes, argued for £30 but was begrudgingly offered only £9.

Lynch, playing the part of a genial guest, brought rum from Gray's Black Horse Inn, ensuring he stayed sober as he plotted his next heinous acts. On a cold night, he lured young John Macnamara out to chop wood, only to murder him with an axe. He cunningly covered up the crime, deceiving the family into thinking John had wandered off.

Bridget's maternal instincts kicked in as her son remained missing, but her growing unease led to a fatal encounter. Lynch, seizing a moment of distraction, killed both her and Mulligan with his axe. The horror escalated when he turned his murderous intent towards 13-year-old Mary. In a chilling confession, Lynch admitted to giving her time to pray before committing an unspeakable act of violence against her.

After this brutal spree, Lynch coldly gathered and burned the bodies of his victims, remarking morbidly on the flames. He then buried the remains, erased evidence by burning clothes, and locked up the hut, concocting a cover-up that involved placing a deceitful notice in the Sydney Gazette and penning fake letters in Mulligan's name.

Assuming the alias 'Dunleavy', Lynch manipulated his way into taking over

Mulligan's lease and hired the unsuspecting Barnetts as laborers, confident in their naivety. When a neighbor, Mr. Gordon, visited, Lynch coolly spun a tale about the family's absence, allaying any immediate suspicions.

Meanwhile, the colonial authorities grew increasingly certain of foul play in the disappearance of several individuals, including the carriers Edmund Ireland and the Aboriginal boy, along with the Fraser father and son. Despite no bodies being found, evidence mounted, and a significant reward was offered for information leading to the capture of the culprits behind these sinister deeds.

Under the guise of John Dunleavy, John Lynch's dark journey continued as he traveled to Sydney on business. On his way back, fate intertwined his path with Kearns Landregan, a 27-year-old working for an innkeeper in Berrima, who had just visited his brother in Stonequarry. Lynch, spotting an opportunity, offered Landregan a six-month fencing job at Wombat Brush for £14, an offer Landregan accepted.

As they journeyed towards Berrima, Lynch's mind turned sinister. He regretted hiring Landregan and plotted to eliminate him, especially after learning that Landregan, known for his sober and frugal ways, had £40 on him. The duo camped near the Ironstone Bridge over the Wingecarribee River, where Lynch executed his grim plan. The next morning, he brutally struck Landregan with a tomahawk while he sat unsuspecting by the fire. He then concealed the body under vegetation and headed to Wombat Brush, planning to return later to bury it.

The following day, George Sturges, a labourer, stumbled upon the grisly scene. The Berrima police were alerted, finding Landregan's severely wounded body, clad only in a shirt adorned with a temperance medal. Identified in Berrima, Landregan's demise sparked an investigation.

John Chalker, a local publican, provided a crucial lead. He recalled seeing a man with Landregan at his Woolpack Inn, and confidently claimed he could identify the murderer. Accompanied by Sergeant Freer and Chief Constable Chapman, Chalker led them to a farm and pointed out Dunleavy, revealing his true identity as John Lynch, a notorious figure with a history of violence dating back to a 1836 trial for a murder at Oldbury Farm.

The discovery of stolen property at the residence and the recognition of a belt belonging to Landregan further implicated Lynch. His reputation as a feared criminal in the district resurfaced, unraveling the mystery of the missing Mulligan family, previously thought to have left suddenly.

Kearns Landregan's life was tragically commemorated with a burial on 24 February 1842 at the All Saints Anglican church in Sutton Forest, marking yet another victim in Lynch's relentless spree of violence and deception.

At the time of his capture, John Lynch was described as a somewhat unassuming figure, standing at a mere five feet three inches with "very small (dark) whiskers" and even considered "rather good looking". By early March, Lynch's true identity was irrefutably confirmed, and he faced formal charges for the murder of Kearns Landregan. His criminal portfolio expanded as suspicions grew about his involvement in the deaths of Edmund Ireland, an Aboriginal boy, and the Frasers (father and son). Investigations also probed the eerie disappearance of John Mulligan and his family. The Sydney Herald's Berrima correspondent expressed a chilling observation: despite his heinous crimes, Lynch's demeanor belied the heart of a cold-blooded murderer.

Following Lynch's arrest, a neighbor, Gordon, recalled an encounter at Mulligan's farm, where Lynch was tending a fire. This tip led the Police Magistrate and officers to a grim discovery at the fire site. Digging through a mound of potatoes, they unearthed human bones and a tooth, thought to belong to a young female. Lynch's cold response to this finding was a defiant denial, suggesting no one could definitively identify the remains as Mulligan's or even confirm they were human.

On 11 March 1842, Lynch faced scrutiny at the Berrima Police Office, linked to the brutal murders of Ireland and the Aboriginal boy. Thomas Cowper, the employer of the deceased, testified that a double-barrelled gun found with Lynch was his property. Additionally, one of Cowper's workers identified clothing items as belonging to Ireland. Cowper, initially hesitant to identify Lynch as the man he had seen on the Liverpool road, later had a moment of recognition upon seeing Lynch's profile, confirming his suspicion. This revelation triggered a vehement outburst from Lynch, who unleashed a torrent of abuse towards Cowper. Subsequently, Lynch was remanded in custody, his fate hanging in the balance as the weight of his crimes and the depth of his deception came to light.

As the Berrima Circuit Court convened on 17 March 1842, with Chief Justice Sir James Dowling presiding, an intriguing affidavit from John Lynch, now known as John Dunleavy, came under scrutiny. Lynch sought access to his alleged property, valued at £276, including a field of potatoes, to fund his legal defense. However, Justice Dowling called the prisoner to court, where Acting Attorney-General Roger Therry raised a pivotal point: Lynch, a convict for life, had no legal right to any property, especially as it was believed to belong to those he was accused of murdering. Consequently, the court denied Lynch's request for funds.

Lynch's trial, held on 21 March 1842, was a spectacle. Charged with the murder of Kearns Landregan, he asserted his right to a fair trial amidst widespread prejudice. Justice Dowling assured him of the jury's respectability. The twelve-hour trial saw a packed courtroom, with attendees from over thirty miles away, including numerous women. Lynch, surprisingly adept, cross-examined witnesses, attempting to sow doubt.

In the late evening, the jury returned a guilty verdict, sealing Lynch's fate.

Two days later, the court reconvened for sentencing. Justice Dowling, donning the black cap, condemned Lynch for his bloodthirsty acts driven by greed, sparing neither the young nor the old. He sentenced Lynch to death by hanging. Lynch, emotionally, claimed the Barnetts, held during the investigation, were innocent, and any misdeeds at his house occurred before their employment.

Amidst this, George Barton, former master at Oldbury Farm and a key witness in Lynch's 1836 murder trial of Thomas Smith, found himself under media scrutiny. An editorial in the Sydney Herald implied Lynch's earlier acquittal was due to Barton's drunkenness in court, leading to the rejection of his testimony. Barton, days before Lynch's execution, penned a letter to the Herald, refuting claims of his intoxication and downplaying his role as a principal witness. He provided affidavits from doctors and witnesses attesting to his health condition, but Justice Burton remained unmoved, leaving the fine for appearing in court in a drunken state unrevoked.

In mid-April, Matthew Ashe from the Sydney Sheriff's Office embarked on a grim journey to Berrima to oversee the executions of John Lynch and Patrick Kleighran (or Clearahan), both condemned for separate murders. Due to the gallows' limitation of accommodating only one individual at a time, a harrowing schedule was set to execute them an hour apart.

Throughout his apprehension and trial, Lynch had stoutly proclaimed his innocence, adamantly refusing to publicly confess his crimes. However, in a dramatic turn on the eve of his execution, Lynch unveiled the full extent of his guilt to Rev. Summers, who had been ministering to him, and later to Police Magistrate George Bowen. His extensive confession, revealing the depth of his atrocities, was later published posthumously.

Despite Bowen having already discovered human remains at Mulligan's farm, Lynch was brought there on the night before his execution. In a chilling admission, he pointed out the burial site of Mulligan, his family, and his other victims.

On the morning of 22 April 1842, Lynch met his end on the temporary gallows behind the new Berrima gaol. Witnesses noted his unflinching composure on the scaffold, his lips moving seemingly without a hint of repentance or remorse for his horrific past.

The tragic aftermath of Lynch's confessions was the discovery of the bodies of the Frasers, father and son, near Cordeaux's Flat, as he had detailed. They were laid to rest on 4 May 1842 in the All Saints Anglican churchyard at Sutton Forest, alongside John Mulligan, Bridget Macnamara, and her children, Mary and John.

Meanwhile, the Berrima Police Magistrate, George Bowen, conducted a relentless search at Razorback for the remains of Edmund Ireland and the Aboriginal boy. Initially, their search seemed futile, leading to speculations that wild dogs might have scavenged the bodies. However, a persistent effort led to the grim discovery of bones on 10 May 1842, described in official records as likely belonging to Cowper's drayman and the Aboriginal boy, tragic victims of Lynch's murderous spree.

Smuttynose Island Murders

I n the rugged coastal waters off the Isles of Shoals, straddling the boundaries of Maine and New Hampshire, Louis Wagner eked out a meager existence as a solitary fisherman. His life took a fortuitous turn when he crossed paths with John Hontvet and his wife Maren, Norwegian immigrants who had made Smuttynose Island their home since 1868. Unlike Wagner, the Hontvets had successfully carved out a prosperous life from these unforgiving seas. John, a man of towering stature with light hair that shimmered under the sun, was a respected figure among the small, close-knit community that seldom numbered more than fifty souls across the islands.

Each day, before the sun cast its first light, John would steer his beloved schooner, the Clara Bella, through the choppy waters to his fishing grounds. There, he would meticulously work his trawl lines, harvesting the bounty of the sea. His routine was as unvarying as the tides: from the fishing grounds, he would sail to the bustling markets in Portsmouth, New Hampshire. After selling his catch, he would replenish his supplies, and then set sail back to his island home. This diligent rhythm of life brought prosperity to the Hontvets, allowing them to enjoy a comfortable existence in their secluded island abode.

John and Maren, ever generous and kind-hearted, took it upon themselves to ensure that Wagner was not left wanting. They not only provided him with food and clothing but also graciously included him in the flourishing business that John had painstakingly built. This gesture of goodwill was a testament to their unwavering faith in humanity and their desire to uplift those around them.

However, the morning of March 6, 1873, unveiled a harrowing truth that shattered the tranquility of their lives. The Hontvets, in their benevolence, had failed to foresee the darkness lurking in the heart of the man they had so selflessly aided. The repayment of their kindness and trust was to be a grim and shocking revelation, a stark contrast to the serene and industrious life they had known on the isolated Smuttynose Island.

Maren Hontvet, petite yet resilient, exuded a warmth and gentleness that became even more pronounced in the company of others. She was the heart of their modest home on Smuttynose Island, a place she infused with care and beauty. Her decorative flair was evident in every corner of their cottage, adorned with vibrant paints and wallpapers that brought life to the otherwise stark surroundings. Maren took particular joy in nurturing an array of plants, which she lovingly arranged on the sunlit window shelves, creating a small oasis in their isolated world.

Despite the contentment they found in their new life, Maren and John often felt a pang of longing for their families back in Norway. Their quaint red house, a stark contrast against the backdrop of weathered fish sheds and the island's bleached rocky ledges, was Maren's pride. However, during the long hours when John was away at sea, her companionship was limited to Ringe, their small, energetic dog. Ringe's playful dashes across the island's treeless expanse, weaving through thickets of wild rose and bayberry, provided a sense of liveliness in an otherwise solitary environment.

It was about two years into their life on Smuttynose that Louis Wagner entered their world. Wagner, a robust 28-year-old Prussian with a thick accent and a dark, muscular build, presented a stark contrast to the small community. He appeared amiable enough to the Hontvets, yet others in the Isles of Shoals harbored a less favorable view of him. Wagner was an enigma, often silent about his past, and there was an unsettling air about him. Some perceived him as a shadowy figure, ever-present in the corner of a room, seemingly engrossed in his own thoughts yet acutely aware of the conversations around him.

Wagner's solitary fishing expeditions took him to the nearby Star, Malaga, and Cedar Islands, connected to Smuttynose by a network of seawalls and breakwaters. Given the proximity of these islands—Smuttynose itself being only half a mile long and slightly narrower—it was inevitable for the Hontvets to frequently cross paths with their neighbor. Over the two years that followed, a bond seemingly akin to that of siblings developed among the trio. This camaraderie, it was believed, had grown as deep and strong as that between brothers and a sister.

The serene life on Smuttynose Island was imbued with renewed joy in May 1871, as Maren Hontvet welcomed her sister, Karen Christensen, from Norway. Karen's arrival, while a source of happiness for Maren, was tinged with sorrow. Karen had left behind a lost love in Norway, a memory that clung to her, casting a shadow of melancholy. Yet, Maren, ever the optimist, believed wholeheartedly that she could help her sister heal and embrace the promise of a new beginning in this remote corner of the world.

Karen soon found employment as a live-in maid with a family on Appledore Island, the largest of the Isles of Shoals. This opportunity marked the start of her journey towards a fresh chapter in her life, away from the pains of the past.

Meanwhile, John Hontvet's fishing business was thriving. In June 1872, he extended an offer of employment to Louis Wagner, who also began living with the Hontvets. Wagner, previously somewhat of an outsider, now seemed to blend seamlessly into the fabric of the Hontvet family, blurring the lines between a hired hand and a member of the household.

However, October of that year brought more changes. John's brother,

Matthew, arrived from Norway to join them on Smuttynose. Accompanying Matthew was another member of Maren's family, her brother Ivan Christensen, and his wife, Anethe. Ivan was a striking figure, tall and well-built, while Anethe was a vision of beauty, with piercing blue eyes, a bright smile, and blonde hair that cascaded down her back, reaching her knees when unbraided. The couple, having been wed since the previous Christmas, brought with them an air of newlywed bliss.

The Hontvets opened their home and hearts to these new arrivals. The cottage, once the domain of John and Maren, now teemed with the energy of five vibrant souls. Ivan and Matthew joined John in his fishing endeavors, while Anethe assisted Maren with the household duties. Wagner, despite the increasing crowding, remained with the Hontvets for five more weeks before departing on the Addison Gilbert, another fishing schooner, leaving Smuttynose in November.

The Hontvets, ever generous, surely felt a sense of accomplishment in having helped Wagner find his footing. Yet, Wagner's fortunes soon took a downward spiral. The Addison Gilbert met with disaster, leaving him to eke out a meager living along the Portsmouth wharves. His financial struggles were evident in his threadbare clothing and worn shoes, and he soon found himself unable to pay rent to the Jonsens, his landlords.

As the harsh winter gave way to the first whispers of spring in March 1873, a sense of normalcy returned to the island. On the morning of March 5, with the promise of a clear sky and favorable winds, John, Matthew, and Ivan set sail, their plans for the day including selling their catch in Portsmouth and purchasing bait from an early train arriving from Boston. Encountering a neighbor at sea, they sent word back to Smuttynose that they wouldn't be returning midday as usual, due to the advantageous sailing conditions, and would instead return later that evening. Unbeknownst to them, this decision would set in motion a series of events that would forever alter the course of their lives and leave an indelible mark on the history of the Isles of Shoals.

As the afternoon shadows lengthened on Smuttynose Island, the message from the men at sea finally reached the women. The supper they had lovingly prepared was ready, but they decided to keep it warm, awaiting the return of their husbands and brother. Karen Christensen, who had been living on the island, was in the midst of a transitional phase in her life. She had recently left her position as a maid and was preparing to move to Boston to start a new chapter as a seamstress. Her stay on Smuttynose was a brief interlude, a chance to spend time with her sister and family before embarking on her new journey.

Meanwhile, in Portsmouth, as the Clara Bella docked in the early evening, Louis Wagner was there, ostensibly to assist with mooring the vessel. His presence, though slightly unusual, didn't raise any immediate concerns. When he inquired about the men's plans to return to Smuttynose, his question seemed odd but not alarming. John Hontvet explained their plans hinged on the timely arrival of the bait; if delayed, they would stay overnight to prepare their lines and return in the morning. Wagner, perhaps seizing an opportunity, offered to help with the laborious task of baiting the lines, a chore that could stretch well into the night. His offer accepted, he soon departed the wharf.

The tranquility of the evening at 7:30, when Wagner was last seen in Portsmouth, belied his sinister intentions. He had somehow ascertained that the bait hadn't arrived, and with his intimate knowledge of John Hontvet's prosperous business, he hatched a desperate and audacious plan to burglarize the Hontvet home. Under the scant illumination of a quarter moon, Wagner covertly commandeered a dory on the Piscataqua River, mere hours after its owner had replaced its worn thole pins. Silently, he rowed past the shadowy brick buildings, their chimneys quietly emitting streams of smoke, and ventured into the harbor, setting a course for the Isles of Shoals. The 12-mile row was a formidable challenge, but Wagner, a seasoned oarsman driven by desperation, was undeterred. His determination was likely fueled by the same dogged resolve that had enabled John Hontvet to make similar solo journeys in a whaling boat numerous times.

Back on Smuttynose, the night wore on and the three women in the Hontvet household eventually conceded that the men would not be returning home that evening. Resigned, they prepared for bed. Maren, ever the considerate hostess, arranged a bed for Karen in the kitchen, where the warmth offered a respite from the chill of the upstairs bedrooms. Maren and Anethe then retreated to an adjacent bedroom, unaware of the dark turn their peaceful evening was about to take.

The night was eerily quiet, the only sound being the crunch of crusty snow under Louis Wagner's boots as he approached the island in his stolen dory. The moon cast a pale light over the landscape, giving the snow a ghostly shimmer. Wagner, with calculated stealth, chose not to land in the cove where the Clara Bella usually anchored. Instead, he rowed to the island's more secluded side, disembarking on the rocky shore that lay shrouded in shadows.

He lurked in the darkness, watching the Hontvets' lone cottage from afar. Hours passed, and eventually, the lights inside the cottage flickered and died, signaling to Wagner that the occupants were likely asleep. Clad in heavy rubber boots that muffled his steps, he ascended the slope towards the house. The cold air was sharp against his skin, but his focus remained unwavering. Reaching the door, he tested it and found it unsecured. It opened silently, allowing him to slip into the kitchen undetected.

In the pitch-black interior, Wagner moved with sinister intent. He quietly jammed a piece of wood into the latch of the bedroom door, where Maren and Anethe lay in unsuspecting slumber. His plan was to conduct his burglary unnoticed, but the unexpected happened – Ringe, the small dog, sensing an intruder, barked loudly, rousing Karen from her sleep.

Startled, Karen called out, mistaking the intruder's silhouette for her brother-in-law. "John? Is that you?" Her voice broke the ominous silence.

From the adjacent room, Maren's voice emerged, tinged with concern.

"Karen? Is something wrong?" she called out, sensing the distress in her sister's voice.

"I thought it was John. He scared me," Karen replied, her voice still heavy with sleep. But before she could comprehend the danger, Wagner struck from the shadows with a chair, delivering a brutal blow. Karen's scream pierced the night, a sound of pure terror.

"Karen! Karen! What's happening?" Maren cried out, panic rising in her voice. She leaped from the bed, desperately pulling at the jammed door. Inside the kitchen, Karen, severely wounded, staggered to her feet, only to be met with another vicious strike from Wagner. Thrown against the bedroom door, she inadvertently freed the latch, tumbling into Maren's arms.

Wagner, relentless in his brutality, charged into the room, swinging wildly and striking both women. In a moment of sheer adrenaline, Maren managed to drag her sister out of Wagner's reach. She quickly shut and barricaded the door, cutting off his access.

Anethe, paralyzed with horror, had witnessed the unfolding nightmare from a corner of the room. "Anethe! Run! Hide!" Maren implored, her voice trembling with fear. Anethe, barely able to process what was happening, clambered out of a window into the freezing night, her feet bare against the snow. She stood motionless, overwhelmed by shock. "Run!" Maren screamed again, her voice desperate. But it was too late; Wagner had abandoned his attempt to break into the room and had exited the house.

As he emerged into the moonlit night, he approached Anethe, his identity now clear in the pale light. "Louis! Louis!" Anethe shrieked, her voice filled with disbelief and terror. The peaceful night on Smuttynose Island had been irrevocably shattered, its tranquility replaced by a scene of unimaginable horror.

The night had spiraled into a realm of unimaginable horror, and Maren Hontvet found herself witnessing a scene so ghastly it defied belief. Through the window, she saw Louis Wagner, a man they had once considered almost family, transformed into a monstrous figure. Anethe stood before him, her hands raised in a futile gesture of defense. Wagner, with chilling resolve, grabbed the long handle of an axe from the woodpile. In a moment that seemed suspended in time, he raised the axe against the backdrop of the star-studded sky and brought it down with lethal force onto Anethe's head. Her body convulsed violently before collapsing, lifeless, as Wagner relentlessly continued his assault. Maren, frozen in shock, was so close to the horrific scene that she felt she could almost touch Wagner's arm.

Realizing that Anethe was beyond help, Maren's thoughts turned desperately to her own survival and that of her sister, Karen. She found Karen kneeling by the bed, disoriented and barely conscious. "Karen! Karen! We must run!" Maren pleaded, but Karen, overwhelmed by her injuries, could barely respond, murmuring only about her exhaustion. Outside, the nightmarish tableau continued as Wagner, having completed his gruesome act, turned his attention back to the bedroom.

Maren, driven by a primal instinct to survive, knew that their chances were slim if they remained together. She quickly wrapped herself in a heavy skirt and, sensing Wagner re-entering the house, made her escape through the window into the snow, stained with the evidence of the night's atrocities. Ringe, eerily silent, followed closely. Her feet were torn by the icy undergrowth as she ran, her mind racing with thoughts of escape. She hoped to find Wagner's boat in the cove but was met with despair when she found it missing. Her initial thought was to hide in the cellar of a nearby vacant building, but she quickly dismissed it, knowing Wagner might anticipate such a move. Instead, she made a desperate dash along the shore to the island's far side, passing the cottage as far as possible. The agonizing sounds of Karen's suffering reached her ears as she huddled between two rocks near the water's edge, clutching Ringe close, the roar of the waves mercifully drowning out the nightmarish sounds from the house.

Inside, Karen attempted a feeble escape through a window, but Wagner, fuelled by a frenzied rage, was upon her. He swung the axe haphazardly, his blows landing with deadly precision before missing and striking the window sill, breaking the handle. Karen's listless body collapsed back into the room. Wagner, undeterred, took a handkerchief, twisted it around her throat, and pulled with ruthless force, ensuring the finality of his ghastly deed. The peaceful island had become a scene of unspeakable violence, a stark contrast to the serene life the Hontvets had once known.

The desperation that gripped Louis Wagner in the aftermath of his heinous acts was palpable. Realizing that Maren had eluded him, his anxiety escalated. The island, once a tranquil haven, became the stage for a frantic and futile search. Wagner left a harrowing trail of blood-soaked footprints in the snow as he scoured each building, driven by the need to eliminate the only witness who could identify him. Time, however, was not on his side. With the cover of darkness as his only ally, he was forced to abandon his search for Maren, knowing that his chances of escape were dwindling.

Returning to the scene of his crime, Wagner dragged Anethe's body into the kitchen, a final act of disrespect to her life. In a bizarre display of normalcy amidst the chaos, he brewed a pot of tea, leaving behind bloodstained fingerprints on the handle, and consumed some food he had brought with him, using utensils from the Hontvets' home. His search through the house yielded a meager $15, a paltry sum for such brutality. Leaving Anethe's lifeless body beside a clock, stopped at 1:07 a.m. during the struggle, he fled the scene of his crimes.

As dawn broke, Maren, still in hiding, was overcome by fear and uncertainty. It was not until eight o'clock in the morning that she mustered the courage to emerge from her hiding place. Her attempts to attract the attention of workers on a nearby island were futile, so she braved the painful journey across the breakwater to Malaga, where she finally caught the attention of Jorge Ingerbredsen's children on Appledore Island. Jorge swiftly rowed to her rescue, bringing her back to the safety of his home before gathering a group of armed men to investigate Smuttynose. What they discovered there was a gruesome testament to Wagner's savagery.

Meanwhile, the Clara Bella was sighted on the horizon, gracefully cutting through the icy sea under the morning sun. Seeing signals from the shore, Matthew and Ivan approached Appledore in a tender, while John sailed the schooner to its mooring at Smuttynose. Upon reaching Appledore, they were met with the vague but ominous news of "some trouble on Smuttynose." They hurried to the Ingerbredsen house, where they found Maren in a state of shock and despair.

Ivan, frantic with worry, demanded to know Anethe's whereabouts. Maren's tearful response left no room for hope: "Anethe is... at home." Ivan and Matthew rushed back to the tender, rowing with a sense of urgency to Smuttynose. They arrived simultaneously with John, and all three hurried to the cottage. The sight that greeted Ivan was heart-wrenching: his beloved Anethe, her golden hair stained with blood, lay motionless on the floor. Overcome with grief, he stumbled outside, collapsing into the snow.

John and Matthew, after taking in the full horror of the scene, returned to the Clara Bella and sailed to Appledore. Later that afternoon, they, along with others, brought Maren's harrowing account of the night's terror to the authorities in Portsmouth, setting in motion the pursuit of a murderer who had shattered the peace of their once-idyllic island life.

The tragic events on Smuttynose Island sent shockwaves throughout the coastal communities. News of the gruesome murders traveled swiftly, propelled by the rapid lines of telegraph. Police stations along the coast were on high alert, with a detailed description of Louis Wagner disseminated far and wide. The story, with all its morbid details, dominated the evening newspapers, capturing the public's horrified fascination.

In a crucial breakthrough, two individuals, both acquainted with Wagner, reported seeing him in Newcastle around six in the morning following the murders. Their accounts were corroborated by the discovery of the stolen dory near a place ominously known as "Devil's Den." The newly installed thole pins on the dory, worn down significantly, testified to the arduous journey Wagner had undertaken.

Wagner, after returning to the Jonsens' residence for a quick change of clothes, boarded a 9 A.M. train to Boston. There, in a seemingly nonchalant manner, he indulged in a shopping spree, buying new boots and clothes. He even spent time socializing with acquaintances at a local boarding house. Thanks to the detailed information provided by John Hontvet about Wagner's frequented spots, Boston police were able to apprehend him that evening. Wagner, dressed in his new attire over his old clothes, offered no resistance upon arrest.

The following day's transfer of Wagner to the Boston depot, en route to Portsmouth, attracted a massive and hostile crowd of around 500 people. This animosity was mirrored at every train station along the journey, with enraged citizens demanding swift justice. Upon his arrival in Portsmouth, a colossal crowd of 10,000 people, fueled by anger and grief, narrowly missed lynching him.

The legal jurisdiction for the trial lay with the state of Maine, and transferring Wagner there proved to be a perilous endeavor. A lynch mob, comprising over 200 fishermen from the islands and the coast, awaited his transfer from Portsmouth jail. Despite the armed escort of police and Marines, the mob, inflamed with a thirst for vengeance, hurled stones and bricks at them.

Louis Wagner's trial began on June 9, 1873. The proceedings, marked by intense public interest, lasted nine days. After a mere 55 minutes of deliberation, the jury returned a guilty verdict. Wagner's subsequent escape from jail was short-lived; he was recaptured in New Hampshire. On June 25, 1875, 27 months post-crime, Wagner was executed by hanging in the yard of the state prison in Thomaston, Maine.

The aftermath of the tragedy left deep scars. Maren and John Hontvet, unable to return to the life they once knew on the Isles of Shoals, relocated to Portsmouth, where John resumed his work as a fisherman. Ivan Christensen, irrevocably haunted by the loss of his beloved Anethe, spent a desolate summer on Appledore Island, working as a carpenter. His demeanor was one of profound grief and detachment, never speaking unless spoken to and avoiding eye contact. At summer's end, he returned to Norway alone, a broken man, and faded into obscurity, his story ending as quietly as it had been tragically altered.

The Servant Girl Annihilator

In the late 19th century, the city of Austin, Texas, underwent a remarkable transformation. By 1885, it had evolved from a quaint cowtown into a bustling urban center with a population of 23,000. This period marked a significant chapter in the city's history, as it began to establish itself as an educational hub, boasting three colleges. It was during this time that the renowned poet O. Henry chose Austin as his abode, adding to the city's growing cultural significance.

However, with urban growth often comes an increase in crime, and Austin was no exception. Within a year, the city was shaken by a series of brutal and mysterious murders that would go down in history as one of the most perplexing unsolved cases. The victims, who were diverse in their backgrounds, included four black servants, an 11-year-old girl, a black man, and two white women. Their deaths in the mid-1880s were the first of their kind in the young city and would remain an unsolved mystery for over a century.

The tale begins on a chilling note in December 1884, just days before the new year. Mollie Smith, a 25-year-old servant working in the household of Walter K. Hall, a Galveston insurance salesman, was living in a modest apartment at the back of Hall's residence at 901 West Pecan Street. She had been employed there for a little over a month and was in a relationship with Walter Spencer, a 30-year-old who shared her living space.

One night, the peace of the Hall household was shattered by Spencer's harrowing screams, pleading for help and claiming he had been attacked. Tom Chalmers, Hall's brother, found Spencer bleeding heavily from multiple head wounds. Spencer, in his agony, mentioned that Mollie was missing.

The following morning, the grim truth was revealed. Mollie's lifeless body was discovered in the backyard, behind an outhouse. She had been brutally attacked, her body bearing a severe head wound, and was found in a state of undress, indicating she had been dragged outside post-mortem.

The crime scene in her bedroom was a tableau of violence: shattered glass, disarrayed furniture, bloody fingerprints, and a bloodied axe, believed to be the murder weapon. This horrific incident baffled investigators, who traditionally sought suspects among those close to the victim, such as estranged lovers or vengeful acquaintances. However, Spencer, having been in a harmonious relationship with Mollie, had no apparent motive.

The police soon apprehended William Brooks, a bartender at the Barrel House Saloon and Mollie's former lover. Despite suspicions stemming from presumed jealousy over her relationship with Spencer, and his history with Mollie in Waco before moving to Austin, Brooks maintained his innocence, claiming an alibi at the time of the murder. He was never prosecuted, leaving the case unsolved and shrouded in mystery.

Brooks, maintaining his innocence, remarked, "They have got hold of the wrong man sure," a statement that echoed through the annals of Austin's history, leaving the haunting mystery of the murders unsolved to this day.

Following the brutal murder of Mollie Smith, a sinister pattern emerged, particularly targeting servant girls. Throughout the spring, the police were inundated with reports of violent home invasions. These attacks predominantly affected black servant girls, but one incident involved a German servant girl who was assaulted with a stone for refusing to hand over money to an intruder.

In March, a particularly alarming incident occurred at the residence of Col. J.H. Pope, located at the intersection of Guadalupe Street and College Avenue. Two Swedish servants reported a harrowing experience where an unknown assailant knocked on their door and, upon being denied entry, fired a shot through the window. The bullet grazed the neck of one girl and struck the other in the shoulder, adding a new level of terror to the escalating series of attacks.

The next significant attack occurred on May 7, 1885. Eliza Shelley, a 30-year-old cook employed by Dr. L.B. Johnson, lived with her three young children in a small cabin behind the doctor's cottage at the corner of San Jacinto and Cypress streets. The morning of the attack, Dr. Johnson returned from the market to find his wife profoundly distressed, informing him that she believed Eliza had been murdered. Mrs. Johnson had heard screams from Eliza's cabin and sent her niece to investigate, only to discover a horrific scene.

Eliza's lifeless body lay on the floor of her cabin, bearing multiple gruesome injuries. She had suffered a deep wound over her right eye, a stab above her ear, and another between her eyes. The blood-stained pillows and sheets, along with the disheveled state of the room, indicated a violent struggle. The murderer had dragged Eliza from her bed and wrapped her in the bedspread, a chilling detail that added to the mystery of the crime.

The investigation yielded few clues. The police found a barefoot track in the dirt, but no weapon was discovered. The only eyewitness, Eliza's eight-year-old son, was in a state of shock. His recollection was vague; he remembered a man with a white rag over his face demanding to know where his mother kept her money. The boy's account was chilling, "He told me to cover up my head. If I didn't, he would kill me," he recounted.

In a desperate bid to find the perpetrator, the police arrested 19-year-old Andrew Williams, who was found barefoot near the crime scene. Another suspect, 30-year-old Ike Plummer, was also arrested based on a neighbor's testimony. The neighbor claimed to have witnessed Plummer and Eliza arguing weeks before her murder and had seen Plummer with either a hammer or a hatchet in his pocket the night of the murder.

Despite these arrests, neither Williams nor Plummer was prosecuted for the murder. The evidence against them was circumstantial at best, and they were eventually released. The mystery of Eliza Shelley's murder, like that of Mollie Smith, remained unsolved, contributing to the growing sense of unease and fear that had begun to envelop the city of Austin.

Just three weeks after the tragic murder of Eliza Shelley, the city was jolted by another horrifying incident. On May 23, the piercing screams of Irene Cross, a 23-year-old servant of Sophia Witman, shattered the relative calm of the neighborhood. The brutality of the attack was shocking: Irene sustained a deep, six-inch gash across her right arm, almost severing it, and a savage slash across her head, starting above her right eye, as if the attacker had attempted to scalp her. She was found outside the Witman residence, desperately crying out for help.

In the brief time before succumbing to her injuries, Irene provided a description of her assailant through her son. She described the intruder as a "big, chunky negro man, barefooted and with his pants rolled up," wearing a brown hat, a ragged coat, and armed with a pocketknife. This disturbing account added another layer of fear and mystery to the series of violent attacks plaguing the city.

The summer months brought no respite from the violence. Austin was besieged by a series of break-ins and assaults targeting servant girls. Shots were fired at them, their quarters were invaded, and large rocks were hurled through their windows in terrifying nocturnal assaults. In one particularly brazen theft, a thief stole jewelry from the home of a servant in the dead of night.

City Marshal Grooms Lee publicly acknowledged the challenges faced by the police force in curbing this wave of crime. "I try to do the best I can with the few men under control," Lee stated. He lamented the inadequacy of their resources, saying, "The trouble is, the force is too small."

One of the most heart-wrenching incidents occurred on a seemingly peaceful Sunday morning. Rebecca Ramey and her 11-year-old daughter Mary were sleeping soundly when an unimaginable horror unfolded. Rebecca was abruptly awakened by a violent blow to her head from a sandbag. She sustained a fractured skull and a deep wound on the left side of her head from a sharp instrument. The situation turned even more tragic when her daughter Mary was dragged into a nearby wash house and brutally assaulted. Her attacker, in a gruesome act of violence, drove an iron pin into both of her ears, penetrating her brain. Mary tragically lived only a short time after the police arrived, succumbing to her injuries and bleeding to death in Weed's backyard.

These relentless and brutal attacks instilled a pervasive sense of fear throughout Austin, as the community struggled to comprehend the motives behind these heinous crimes and the identity of the assailant or assailants responsible.

The mysterious and violent events that plagued Austin in 1885 continued to unfold with a series of chilling incidents. One such event involved Weed, who recounted waking up around 5 a.m. to what he described as an "unnatural sound," akin to a dog howling. Upon investigating, he encountered Rebecca, who was in a state of distress and claimed she was feeling sick. This interaction marked the beginning of another grim chapter in the city's ongoing saga of violence.

The investigation led the police to use dogs, which followed a scent to a nearby stable. This discovery resulted in the arrest of Tom Allen. However, Allen's involvement was later questioned by a doctor, casting doubt on his guilt. Alex Mack was another individual rumored to be involved in the crime, but the police did not arrest him, leaving the community in a state of uncertainty and fear.

The Austin Daily Statesman, a local newspaper, was vocal in its criticism of the city's law enforcement during this period of unrest. In September, the Statesman published a scathing article, accusing the city marshal of corruption and incompetence in managing the police force. The paper went as far as to suggest that the murders were "cunningly planned, carefully directed and intelligently consummated," implying that the individuals arrested thus far did not fit the profile of such a calculated criminal.

Furthermore, the Statesman criticized the city government for its inefficiency in addressing the escalating crime, stating that Austin's crime rate was alarmingly high, "second to no place in the civilized world." This indictment of the city's governance and law enforcement added to the growing public discontent and fear.

Up until the end of September, it appeared that women were the primary targets of the elusive killer. However, the nature of the crimes took an even darker turn on September 28. In a shocking incident, a couple, Gracie Vance and Orange Washington, along with two of their friends, Lucinda Boddy and Patsy Gibson, were attacked in the middle of the night.

William B. Dunham, the owner of the property at 2408 San Marcos Street where Gracie and Orange lived, recounted being awakened by disturbing noises that he initially thought were caused by Orange assaulting Gracie, a sadly frequent occurrence. However, around 1 a.m., he was startled awake again by a sound that seemed like someone jumping through the window of his servants' cabin, followed by a woman's scream.

Armed with his gun, Dunham rushed to investigate and found Lucinda fighting with a man outside his front gate. In the ensuing struggle, Lucinda grabbed Dunham, preventing him from firing at the assailant. "My God, Mr. Dunham, we are all dead!" she exclaimed in terror.

The police were called by Dunham's neighbor, and some neighbors even attempted to shoot at the fleeing attacker. Notably, the assailant left behind a horse, saddled and bridled, hitched to a tree near Dunham's house, a curious detail that added to the mystery of these harrowing events.

The night of the attack on Gracie Vance, Orange Washington, Lucinda Boddy, and Patsy Gibson at 2408 San Marcos Street in Austin was a scene of unimaginable horror. The details that emerged painted a picture of brutality and chaos.

Gracie, a young woman of 20, was discovered about 75 yards away from the cabin, her body bearing the marks of a savage assault. The attacker had not only hit her but also dragged her out of the cabin window, over a fence, and then committed the heinous act of rape before mercilessly beating her to death with a rock. The numerous gashes across her face and head testified to the ferocity of the attack.

Orange, aged 25, was found inside the cabin, lying on the floor between the bed and the open window. His head was nearly severed in two by a deep gash that reached down to his skull. Tragically, he was still breathing when discovered, but his injuries were too severe, and he did not survive long.

William B. Dunham, the property owner, recounted a chilling discovery: an ax, smeared with blood and hidden under the blankets in the bedroom. According to Dunham, this ax was a foreign object on his property, as neither he nor anyone else there owned such a tool.

Lucinda and Patsy, both suffering from head injuries, had been sleeping on the cabin floor when they were attacked. The intruder had used a sandbag to incapacitate Lucinda before leaping through the window, which explained the noise that had startled Dunham earlier. Lucinda told the police that she recognized the attacker as Doc Woods, a known acquaintance of Gracie and possibly Orange. Dunham corroborated this by testifying that he had seen Woods at the cabin previously.

Lucinda's account of the attack was harrowing. After being hit, she managed to light a lamp and confronted Woods, pleading with him, "Oh, Doc, don't do it!" She then saw the blood and repeated her plea. Woods, according to Lucinda, ordered her to extinguish the light, saying, "Don't look at me. Blow out that light."

In the wake of the attack, police arrested Oliver Townsend and Doc Woods. Woods was wearing a bloody shirt at the time of his arrest, though it was later determined that the blood was not related to the crime. Additionally, Netherly Overton, the owner of the horse found at the murder scene, was arrested. Overton claimed his stepson had taken the horse and left it hitched nearby while he went to a store, but it had been stolen.

The case took another twist with the testimony of Johnson Trigg, who claimed to have overheard Townsend and Woods plotting Gracie's murder. According to Trigg, Woods had expressed hesitation about proceeding that night, to which Townsend allegedly responded with a chilling declaration of intent to kill Gracie. Trigg also claimed to have heard Townsend discussing plans to kill Rebecca Ramey before her daughter Mary's murder. However, Trigg's credibility was later called into question, leading to his sentencing for perjury.

The perplexing series of murders in Austin during 1885 continued to baffle both the authorities and the public. The suspects, Doc Woods, Oliver Townsend, and Netherly Overton, faced intense scrutiny but ultimately were not prosecuted for the crimes.

Doc Woods provided an alibi, claiming he was visiting a Mr. Baird on the Sunday of the murder and didn't leave until 10 p.m. He insisted that he went home afterward and slept until the early hours of the next day, when he had to get up for cotton picking. Townsend's alibi was less concrete; he mentioned leaving church around 9 p.m. that Sunday night but admitted he had no one to corroborate his whereabouts except his mother.

Patsy, a key witness, recounted a disturbing incident occurring a few nights before the murder. She testified that Woods had approached the cabin when she was alone with Gracie. He asked to be let in, but they refused him entry. Gracie, sensing danger, instructed Patsy to fetch a gun and check who was at the window. Woods identified himself and insisted on staying the night, but was again denied entry by Gracie. Lucinda added that on the night of the murder, Woods had again appeared at the window.

Despite these alarming testimonies, the authorities did not prosecute Woods, Townsend, or Overton.

In response to the ongoing mystery, City Marshal Grooms Lee, in an October 7 speech, acknowledged that the murders remained unsolved and proposed expanding the police force. This force had previously been limited to a marshal, a sergeant, and twelve policemen. The city council responded by passing an ordinance to offer a reward for the arrest and conviction of anyone responsible for the murders and authorized the mayor to hire detectives for further investigation.

Later in October, Lee and other investigators arrested Alex Mack after an altercation at the Black Elephant Saloon. Mack accused Lee and his officers of excessive force, alleging they had nearly lynched him. Lee, however, dismissed these claims, stating that he had substantial reasons to believe Mack was involved in the murder of Mary Ramey.

Mack's incarceration lasted nine days before he was released. Throughout November, several other names emerged in connection with the Ramey murder, including James Thompson, Cullen Crocket, and Richard Bacon, but none led to substantial progress in the case. In a twist, Walter Spencer, previously acquitted in the murder of Mollie Smith, was arrested again but quickly released after another acquittal.

The Austin Daily Statesman captured the public sentiment, writing, "The crimes still remain a mystery, and their guilty authors retain the secret...This seems to be a year unprecedented in the character of crimes." This statement echoed the frustration and fear gripping Austin, as the city grappled with a series of unsolved crimes, each more baffling and brutal than the last.

The year 1885 in Austin, Texas, had been marred by a series of heinous crimes, primarily targeting women. Until Christmas Eve, these attacks had seemed to spare the city's white population. However, on the night of December 24, a harrowing incident shattered any illusion of safety, as two white women fell victim to brutal violence, marking a chilling escalation in the nature of the crimes that had been terrorizing Austin.

Susan Hancock lived on East Water Street with her husband, Moses, a mechanic. Described as a beautiful woman with an Eastern states' upbringing, she was home alone that fateful night. Their daughters were out at a Christmas party, and with their expected late return, the house was left unlocked in a quiet, unsuspecting state.

The tranquility of the night was shattered when Moses Hancock awoke with a sense of alarm, intuitively feeling that something was amiss in their home. His disorientation intensified when he realized his pants were missing, an oddity that propelled him to check on his wife. He entered her room, illuminated by moonlight, only to be met with a horrifying sight. The bed was splattered with clots of blood, but Susan was nowhere to be found. Initially suspecting a robbery, his worst fears were confirmed when police later discovered an ax at the scene.

In a state of panic, Hancock rushed outside and found his wife lying in the backyard, grievously injured and surrounded by a pool of blood. She had been dragged nearly 100 feet from her room. Frantically, he carried her back to the house, calling for help. Neighbors assisted in moving Susan to the parlor, where doctors attended to her critical injuries. She had two skull fractures and was bleeding from her ears.

As police began their investigation, based on Hancock's account of seeing two men jump his fence, bloodhounds were released to track the suspects. Yet, no conclusive evidence was found.

Meanwhile, at the residence of architect James Phillips Sr. on West Hickory Street, another tragedy was unfolding. The household was jolted awake just after midnight by the younger Phillips calling out for help. The scene in their bedroom was one of horror: blood-soaked sheets and pillows, and James Phillips Jr. lying injured with a deep head wound, an ax lying ominously beside the bed. Eula Phillips, James's wife, was missing. Their child, spared from harm, lay in the bloodstained bed.

A gruesome trail of blood led to the yard, where Eula was discovered lifeless near the fence. Her body was naked, with a piece of wood laid across her chest and arms, her hands outstretched, surrounded by her own blood. The brutality of her attack was evident: she had been assaulted, dragged outside, raped, and murdered.

The aftermath of the chilling Christmas Eve murders in 1885 Austin was marked by a frenzied response from the authorities. In the ensuing days, the city's law enforcement, under the direction of City Marshal James Lucy, intensified their efforts to apprehend the perpetrator or perpetrators. This led to the arrest of nearly a dozen black men, reflecting the tense racial dynamics of the time.

Marshal Lucy issued a directive to the police force, instructing them to interrogate any man they encountered after a certain hour at night. If an individual could not provide a satisfactory explanation for their whereabouts, they were given 24 hours to leave the city. In a bid to control the situation, the city council mandated that all saloons and liquor stores close at midnight, and appointed thirty additional policemen to the force. They even suggested stationing an officer on every street corner to enhance surveillance and security.

Amidst this heightened atmosphere, various theories circulated about the identity and motives of the killer or killers. One particularly sensational suggestion was that the murders were being committed by an escapee from the insane asylum, who would commit the crimes and then return undetected.

The police, desperate for leads, arrested individuals based on seemingly circumstantial evidence, such as possessing bloody clothes. This included the arrest of a man from San Antonio who boasted about his association with Doc Woods and their supposed attacks in Austin. The newspapers, seeking patterns in the chaos, began speculating about the lunar phases during the murders.

In a significant development, Governor John Ireland announced a reward of $300 for information leading to the arrest and conviction of those involved in the Hancock and Phillips murders. This was later supplemented by additional rewards of $1,000 each for arrests in both cases, as well as for the other murders.

The investigation took a shocking turn on January 2, when James Phillips Jr., still critically injured, was arrested for the murder of his wife, Eula. Moses Hancock was also apprehended but was soon released as the case against him was dismissed.

Phillips' preliminary hearing in February was a crowded affair, with around 60 witnesses testifying about the couple's turbulent relationship and Phillips' demeanor. Despite his frail condition, Phillips himself testified, painting a picture of marital discord and suspicion.

The trial in May was a sensational event, filled with rumors and allegations. The prosecution depicted Eula as an unfaithful wife and Phillips as a jealous husband. Surprising claims surfaced, including one where Eula's sister, Della Campbell, accused George McCutcheon of threatening violence and involvement in a scandalous matter with Eula.

A dramatic moment in the trial involved Phillips carrying a 170-pound man to demonstrate the mismatch between his footprint and the bloody footprint at the crime scene. However, the testimony of Annie Dyer, who claimed to have heard Phillips threaten to kill her, and a police sergeant's account of his dog's behavior, added to the suspicion against Phillips. A doctor even suggested that Phillips' head wound could have been self-inflicted.

After a sensational and tumultuous trial, Phillips was found guilty of second-degree murder and sentenced to seven years in state jail.

The saga of the 1885 Austin murders took a dramatic turn more than six months after James Phillips Jr. was convicted. His conviction was overturned by a court of appeals, which cited significant errors in the trial proceedings. The court highlighted two major flaws: firstly, the inappropriate admission of evidence regarding the unchastity of Phillips' wife without establishing that Phillips was aware of it, and secondly, the consideration of inconsequential and conditional threats made by Phillips, which lacked any real intention of being carried out.

Despite the initial success of the Phillips trial, the decision's reversal coincided with renewed suspicion falling on Moses Hancock, Susan Hancock's husband. Following his wife's death and his daughters' departure, Hancock had moved in with his brother-in-law, W.T. Scaggs. His behavior during this period, particularly his excessive drinking and rambling, became a source of contention within the Scaggs household. Mrs. Scaggs openly expressed her disdain for Hancock's conduct, especially when he was under the influence of alcohol.

In an undercover operation, the police enlisted Joe Gassaway, another boarder at the Scaggs residence, to surveil Hancock for any information related to the murder. During this period, Hancock made a startling admission while intoxicated. He claimed to have seen two men with his wife on the night of the murder, one of whom was carrying her. According to Hancock, when he confronted the man, the other pointed a pistol at him and threatened him.

The preliminary hearing in June 1886 featured testimonies from Susan's sisters, who spoke about Hancock's abusive and drunken behavior towards his wife. Their daughter, Lena, further revealed that her mother had contemplated leaving Hancock, fearing for her life.

The trial began on May 30, 1887, with testimonies from various individuals, including neighbors, police officers, and Hancock's in-laws. The prosecution's strategy was to establish Hancock as the sole individual at the crime scene and thus the only possible perpetrator. However, the defense aimed to prove the presence of others at the house and Hancock's sobriety.

The trial was marked by conflicting testimonies, including one from Tom Glass, a neighbor, who recounted Susan Hancock's fear of her husband and his refusal to leave the house despite her pleas. The defense's argument was weakened when it was revealed that Hancock had been drinking on the night of the murders.

The jury was divided in their verdict, leading to the dismissal of the case. As a result, no one was ever convicted for any of the eight murders, leaving the case shrouded in mystery and speculation for over a century.

A significant development occurred with the death of Nathan Elgin, a black man, in February 1886. Elgin was killed by a policeman while allegedly attempting to abduct a woman. Interestingly, Elgin had a missing pinky toe, which matched a footprint found at the Ramey murder scene. Despite this compelling evidence, Elgin's potential involvement in the murders was not publicly considered until the Hancock trial in 1887. The sheriff noted that no further murders had occurred following Elgin's death and Oliver Townsend's imprisonment.

Elgin's past behavior, including a fight near the governor's mansion and a threatening note to a deputy sheriff, was retrospectively scrutinized, suggesting a possible alignment with the crimes' modus operandi. Following Elgin's death, the horrifying sequence of murders in Austin ceased, leaving a haunting silence and an enduring enigma in the city's history.

The enigma of the 1885 Austin murders continues to captivate and perplex even 129 years later, with new theories and speculations emerging over time.

One of the more prominent theories suggests Nathan Elgin as the likely perpetrator. This theory gains traction from the fact that Elgin had a missing pinky toe, corresponding to a footprint found at the Ramey murder scene, and the cessation of the murders shortly before Elgin's death. J.R. Galloway, an employee of the University of Texas Libraries and the compiler of "The Servant Girl Murders," a comprehensive collection of newspaper articles from the 1880s documenting these crimes, supports this theory. Galloway believes Elgin's profile aligns well with the circumstances and timing of the murders.

Another intriguing, albeit more speculative theory, draws a connection between the so-called Servant Girl Annihilator in Austin and the infamous Jack the Ripper in London. This theory, fueled by the poetic imagination of O. Henry, who resided in Austin at the time, suggests a shared identity between these two killers. The theory is bolstered by the movements of a Malay cook named Maurice, who worked at the Pearl House in Austin and vanished in 1886, around the time the Austin murders ceased. Ripperologists point to similar murders in locations frequented by cargo ships, like Nicaragua, Tunis, and Jamaica, inferring a traveling murderer possibly working on these ships.

These theories, despite their varied plausibility, highlight the enduring intrigue surrounding these crimes. The sheer brutality and graphic nature of the murders make it difficult to reconcile them with the Austin of the 1880s, a city just beginning to take shape. As Galloway notes, these murders were unique in their execution and the mystery surrounding them. Unlike typical violent crimes of the era, which often stemmed from escalated disputes or public altercations, these murders occurred clandestinely, at night, targeting vulnerable individuals. This deviation from the norm led to initial suspicions being cast on those close to the victims, such as husbands or lovers, as the police struggled to conceive of a motive or perpetrator beyond the immediate circle.

The historical significance of these murders, as Dale Flatt, a retired firefighter and volunteer with Save Austin Cemeteries, points out, is undeniable. They form a pivotal part of Austin's history, with most victims, including the unmarked graves of the black victims and Susan Hancock, resting in Oakwood Cemetery. Flatt emphasizes the importance of engaging the public with this history, through initiatives like the Murder, Mayhem and Misadventure walking tours of Oakwood Cemetery, which highlight these and other historical narratives of Austin.

When asked about his theory on the perpetrator, Flatt humorously remarks, "Maybe when I cross over to the other side, I'll find out." This light-hearted response underscores the reality that, despite numerous theories and speculations, the true identity of the murderer or murderers remains a matter of conjecture, leaving us to wonder and hypothesize about one of the most mysterious and chilling chapters in Austin's history.

The Villisca Murders

I n the serene, picturesque town of Villisca, Iowa, a community steeped in the quiet rhythms of rural life, an unspeakable tragedy unfolded over a century ago, casting a long shadow over the small town's history. This dreadful event occurred in a seemingly idyllic home on a peaceful residential street. The walls of this house, once a symbol of familial security, became silent guardians of a dark secret. They bore witness to the brutal murder of the Josiah Moore family and two young guests on the fateful night of June 10, 1912. Even after so many years, these walls not only conceal the identity of the merciless murderer but also seem to be a sanctuary for several paranormal entities that linger, echoing the horror of that night.

Villisca, nestled in the rolling hills of southwest Iowa, is a small, tight-knit community with a population of about 1,300 today. However, in the early 20th century, it was a thriving railroad hub, bustling with activity. In those days, the town's lifeblood was the frequent arrival and departure of more than two dozen passenger and freight trains at its depot. The town was a hive of activity, boasting several hotels, restaurants, stores, theaters, and manufacturing businesses. It was in this vibrant setting that Josiah B. Moore, a prominent figure in the community, made his mark. As the owner and operator of the Moore Implement Company, a franchise of the renowned John Deere Company, he was a formidable presence in the local business landscape. Josiah, known affectionately as "J.B." to those close to him, wed Sarah Montgomery on December 6, 1899, in a ceremony at her parents' home. The couple was blessed with four children – Herman, Katherine, Boyd, and

Paul – and together they navigated the joys and challenges of family life.

J.B. and Sarah were pillars of the Villisca community, actively involved in the local Presbyterian Church and known for their friendly and helpful demeanor. They were well-regarded by their neighbors for their kindness and community spirit. On June 9, 1912, a Sunday, the Moore and Stillinger families attended church together. That evening, a special annual event, the "Children's Day Program," was held, organized by Sarah Moore. It was a joyful community gathering, celebrating the innocence and promise of the young. During this event, Katherine Moore, aged nine, extended an invitation for a sleepover to her friends, Lena Stillinger, aged 12, and her younger sister, Ina May, who was seven. The girls, thrilled at the prospect of spending the night with their friend, eagerly accepted. The program concluded around 9:30 p.m., and the Moore family, along with the Stillinger sisters, made their way home, arriving between 9:45 and 10:00 p.m., unaware of the horror that awaited them.

The next day, the quietude of the Moore residence caught the attention of their neighbor, Mary Peckham. Accustomed to the daily hustle and bustle of the Moore household, she found the silence and stillness unsettling. Concerned, she approached the house between 7:00 and 8:00 a.m., knocking on the door but receiving no response. Finding the door locked, her worry intensified. In a bid to alleviate her concerns, she called upon Josiah's brother, Ross Moore. Upon his arrival, Ross attempted to rouse the household by knocking loudly and calling out, but to no avail. He peered through the windows, only to find them obscured by drawn curtains or covered panes. With a growing sense of dread, he used his keys to enter the home. What he discovered inside was so horrifying that he immediately emerged, urging Mary Peckham to contact the sheriff. The tranquility of Villisca was shattered, and the mystery of who committed this heinous crime continues to perplex and haunt the town to this day.

Ross Moore's discovery of the brutal murder of his brother's family and their two young guests sent shockwaves through the once peaceful community. In the upstairs master bedroom, the lifeless bodies of 43-year-old Josiah Moore and his wife, 39-year-old Sara Moore, were found. They had been mercilessly bludgeoned in their sleep, their bed linens soaked with blood, telling a tale of unimaginable horror. The adjoining rooms revealed further heartbreak - the Moore children, 11-year-old Herman, 10-year-old Mary Katherine, 7-year-old Boyd, and 5-year-old Paul, all shared the same tragic fate, their young lives brutally ended as they slept.

The violence extended to the main level guest room, where the bodies of the Stillinger sisters, 12-year-old Lena and 8-year-old Ina, lay lifeless, having been killed in the same horrific manner as the Moore family. The serene small-town setting was now the backdrop for an unspeakable tragedy.

As Villisca City Marshall Hank Horton and other law enforcement officers arrived at the scene, the gruesome discovery quickly became the talk of the town. The news spread rapidly, igniting a morbid curiosity among the townspeople. In no time, the Moore residence was inundated with neighbors and onlookers, drawn to the scene by a mix of shock, disbelief, and a grim fascination. The crime scene, crucial for gathering evidence, was irreparably compromised as up to a hundred people reportedly wandered through the house. It wasn't until the Villisca National Guard arrived around noon that the area was finally secured and cordoned off.

The ensuing investigation painted a chilling picture of the events. It was determined that the eight victims were killed shortly after midnight. All but Lena Stillinger were believed to have been asleep at the time of the attack. Lena's body, however, bore signs of a struggle, including a defensive wound on her arm, suggesting she had bravely attempted to fend off her assailant. The brutality of the attack was evident from the gouge marks on the ceilings of the parents' and children's bedrooms - grim evidence of the force with which the axe was wielded.

The murder weapon, a bloody axe, was discovered in the guest bedroom where the Stillinger girls were found. It was Josiah Moore's axe, with evidence of an attempt to clean it. A sinister detail emerged: all the curtains in the house had been drawn, and windows without curtains were covered with clothing, as if the killer wanted to conceal his actions from the outside world.

After committing the gruesome acts, the killer covered the victims' faces with bed linens or clothing, a gesture that hinted at a chilling sense of post-mortem remorse or a macabre ritual. Further adding to the eerie scene, investigators found a pan of bloody water on the kitchen table and a plate of uneaten food, suggesting the killer lingered in the house after the murders.

The community was in a state of shock and fear. Initially, locals speculated that a deranged transient must be responsible for such a heinous crime. Posses were quickly formed, with townspeople taking to horseback and automobiles, scouring the city's alleys, and searching every barn, shed, and outhouse in the vicinity, desperate to find the blood-soaked perpetrator. Yet, despite their fervent efforts, they returned without a suspect, leaving the town enveloped in a cloud of fear, suspicion, and unanswered questions.

As night fell in the days following the gruesome discovery, the terror grew. Families, gripped by the fear of a roaming madman, banded together with their neighbors, keeping vigil throughout the night, shotguns at the ready. Windows were no longer just windows; they were vulnerabilities, hastily nailed shut to keep out the unseen threat. The town, once a place of neighborly trust, transformed almost overnight. Locks and weapons sold out in local stores as residents armed themselves, no longer certain of safety in their own homes. Suspicion wormed its way into the community, eroding the bonds between neighbors as eyes narrowed and whispers of doubt and accusation spread like wildfire.

The sensational nature of the murders drew scores of newspaper reporters and private detectives to Villisca, eager to uncover a story in the midst of tragedy. Bloodhounds were brought in to track the scent of the killer, and law enforcement agencies from neighboring counties and states joined the frantic search. This collective effort, while impressive in its scale, only served to underscore the chaos and confusion that had enveloped the town. The murders not only took eight innocent lives but also fractured the once close-knit community, leaving an indelible mark on the town's psyche.

The investigation into the murders cast a wide net, exploring various theories. One such theory considered the possibility of a serial killer, drawing parallels to a string of similar murders that had occurred in the Midwest the previous year. In the fall of 1911, horrifying incidents of entire families being slaughtered in their beds had been reported every two weeks. These chilling events included the murders of the Burnhams and the Waynes in Colorado Springs in September, a family in Monmouth, Illinois, shortly thereafter, and the Showman family in Ellsworth, Kansas, on October 15, 1911. Then, eerily close to the Villisca tragedy, another family was murdered in Paola, Kansas, on June 5, 1912. Despite the striking similarities in these cases, the serial killer theory gradually lost traction and was eventually relegated to the background of the investigation.

Suspicion also fell on transients and strangers passing through Villisca. One such individual was Andy Sawyer, a nomadic laborer who had found temporary work with the Burlington Railroad on the morning of the murders. Sawyer's behavior and circumstances raised eyebrows; he seemed overly interested in the news of the murders, slept fully clothed with an axe within reach, and was considered a loner by his peers. His own comments about being in Villisca on the night of the murders and fears of being a suspect only added to the suspicion surrounding him. This culminated in an unsettling incident where Sawyer, seemingly in a state of agitation, mimed striking motions with an axe, muttering a chilling threat to himself.

Thomas Dyer, the foreman of the rail crew, alarmed by Sawyer's behavior, turned him over to the sheriff on June 18, 1912. Despite the initial suspicion and Sawyer's frequent mention in Grand Jury testimonies, he was eventually ruled out as a suspect. His alibi for the night of the murders was solid; he had been arrested for vagrancy in Osceola, Iowa, at 11:00 p.m. that night.

As the dark cloud of the Villisca axe murders loomed over the small Iowa town, the investigation began to focus more intently on members of the local community, leading to the emergence of several potential suspects. The intensity of the investigation and the swirling rumors began to deeply affect the social fabric of Villisca. The townspeople, once unified in their grief and shock, now found themselves divided, their allegiances and suspicions tearing at the seams of long-standing friendships. Lines were drawn, and the community fractured, as individuals began to identify themselves by whom they suspected of the heinous crime. Relationships strained under the weight of suspicion and accusation, some breaking beyond repair.

Among the first to fall under scrutiny was Sarah Moore's brother-in-law, Lee Van Gilder, who had been married to Sarah's sister, Mary. Known for his violent tendencies and past legal troubles, Van Gilder shared a tumultuous history with the Moore family, marked by animosity and conflict. However, despite the initial suspicion and the apparent motive stemming from familial discord, Van Gilder was eventually exonerated, his name cleared from the list of suspects.

The investigation then pivoted to explore possible motives linked to professional rivalries. Attention turned to Frank F. Jones, a figure well-known in Villisca as both a prominent businessman and an Iowa State Senator. Jones' history with Josiah Moore was marred by bitter competition. Josiah, once a top salesman at Jones' hardware and implement store, left in 1907 to establish his own business. In doing so, he not only became a direct competitor to Jones but also took with him the lucrative John Deere franchise, a move that deeply soured their relationship. The rivalry grew so intense that by 1910, the two men would pointedly avoid each other, even crossing the street to evade any interaction.

While the investigators doubted that Jones would personally commit such a crime, they began to explore the possibility of him hiring a hitman. This line of inquiry led them to William Mansfield, a suspect identified through a tip suggesting that Senator Jones might have contracted him to eliminate the Moore family. In July 1916, Mansfield was apprehended in Kansas City, Kansas, and extradited to Iowa to face a Montgomery County Grand Jury. The local sentiment was heavily against Mansfield, with many anticipating that he would be indicted. However, the jury ultimately declined to indict him, as his alibi held up under scrutiny.

Meanwhile, Frank Jones, although he lost his subsequent bid for re-election as a senator, was never formally charged with any crime related to the murders. The shadow of the Villisca axe murders continued to hang heavily over the community, the unsolved case a constant reminder of the divisions, suspicions, and fears that had been sown in its wake.

The investigation into the Villisca axe murders, a case that had already entangled various members of the community in a web of suspicion, turned its gaze towards a more unlikely suspect: Reverend George Kelly. A traveling minister, Kelly had been present in Villisca for the Children's Day services at the Presbyterian church attended by the Moore family on June 9, 1912. Kelly, a diminutive, twitchy man with an unsettling demeanor, had garnered a dubious reputation. Rumors swirled about his mental instability and possible unsavory interests, particularly toward children. His hasty departure from Villisca on the morning following the murders did not initially arouse suspicion.

However, what drew the authorities' attention to Kelly was his peculiar fixation on the murders. This fixation manifested itself in a barrage of long, rambling letters that Kelly penned to state and local investigators, private detectives, and even to the bereaved families of the victims. His correspondence betrayed an unsettling preoccupation with the grisly details of the case.

Kelly's return to Villisca two weeks after the murders only deepened the suspicion. He deliberately extended his stay to visit the scene of the crime, a move that struck many as morbidly curious at best. As investigators dug deeper into Kelly's background, they uncovered a slew of alarming behaviors: instances of peering into women's bedrooms, nocturnal prowling in various towns, and inappropriate requests to young women to pose nude for him. Moreover, they discovered that Kelly had sent a blood-stained shirt to a laundry service shortly after the murders, a detail that raised serious questions about his involvement.

In April 1917, Kelly was arrested, and as his trial approached, state officials made a concerted effort to extract a confession. After a prolonged interrogation session, Kelly, under duress, dictated a confession on August 31, 1917. In this confession, he claimed to have been compelled by a divine voice to commit the murders after observing the Stillinger girls through a window. However, the trial, which commenced on September 4, 1917, ended inconclusively with a hung jury, and a subsequent trial in November resulted in Kelly's acquittal.

The perception of Kelly's guilt was further complicated by a prevailing theory among Montgomery County residents. Many believed that Kelly was a pawn in a larger conspiracy orchestrated by Frank Jones, a theory fueled by the notion that Jones had used his wealth and influence to manipulate the jury.

Simultaneously, another suspect emerged: Henry Lee Moore (no relation to Josiah Moore). Henry was convicted months after the Villisca murders for killing his mother and grandmother with an axe. His crimes bore striking similarities to the Villisca case, as well as to other axe murders in Colorado Springs, Colorado, and Ellsworth and Paola, Kansas. The pattern suggested the work of a serial killer, yet definitive proof linking Henry Lee Moore to all these crimes remained elusive.

As 1917 drew to a close, the authorities, having exhausted their leads and resources, abandoned their pursuit of the murderer. The Villisca axe murders, a case that had once gripped the nation with its brutality and mystery, faded into unresolved infamy. The killer, whoever they were, evaded justice, leaving a haunting legacy in the small Iowa town. The Murder House, as it came to be known, still stands in Villisca, a grim reminder of the unsolved tragedy.

Following the Moore family's tragic end, the house changed hands eight times, each owner seemingly unable to settle within its unsettling atmosphere. It was not until 1994 that Darwin and Martha Linn took ownership. By this time, the house had severely deteriorated, almost to the point of being condemned. However, the Linns saw past the decay and undertook the arduous task of restoring the house to how it would have appeared in 1912. Their efforts were rewarded in 1998 when the house was officially listed on the National Register of Historic Places.

Today, the Villisca Axe Murder House is open to the public, offering both daytime tours and overnight stays for those curious or brave enough to explore its haunting past. The house's reputation as a hotbed of paranormal activity has earned it a notorious ranking among America's most haunted places.

Over the years, residents and visitors have reported a myriad of ghostly occurrences. People have claimed to see the apparition of a man wielding an axe at the foot of their beds, witnessed ghostly images of blood-stained shoes, and heard the chilling sounds of children crying. Reports of closet doors swinging open without human intervention, and clothes being mysteriously pulled from drawers and closets, only add to the house's eerie ambiance.

One particularly unsettling account came from a visitor who, while sharpening a knife, felt it suddenly turn and stab him in the thumb, as if an unseen hand had taken control. In another instance, a terrified family reportedly fled the house in the middle of the night, never to return.

The house's opening to the public has led to numerous paranormal investigations, many claiming to have captured evidence of supernatural activity through audio recordings, videos, and photographs. A notable investigation by the Ghost Adventures Crew of the Travel Channel allegedly recorded a voice claiming responsibility for the murders, chillingly stating, "I killed six kids."

Visitors often report uncanny experiences, such as hearing children's voices in empty rooms, unexplained whispers, and the sounds of objects moving or falling without apparent cause. The attic, believed to be the hiding spot of the murderer on that fateful night, is particularly notorious for its oppressive and malevolent atmosphere. One visitor recounted being physically barred by an unseen force from entering the attic.

While many are convinced of the house's haunting, there are skeptics too, including former residents who claim never to have experienced anything out of the ordinary. The Villisca Axe Murder House thus stands as a monument to both a tragic piece of history and a continuing source of mystery and intrigue. For those seeking to unravel its secrets, the house remains open, inviting visitors to step inside and judge for themselves whether the spirits of the past still linger within its walls.

Axeman of New Orleans

For a period stretching over a year, from May 1918 to October 1919, the vibrant city of New Orleans in Louisiana was gripped by terror, haunted by the shadow of a ruthless serial killer who came to be known as the "Axeman." This reign of terror began on a chilling note with the brutal murder of an Italian grocer, Joseph Maggio, and his wife, Catherine, on May 23, 1918. The unsuspecting couple were viciously attacked in their sleep, in their modest apartment situated above their grocery store. The killer, with cold precision, slit their throats using a straight razor, following up this heinous act by gruesomely bashing their heads with an ax. This horrifying scene marked the beginning of a series of blood-curdling events that would leave the city in a state of paranoia and fear.

The investigation into the Maggios' murders unveiled a sinister clue: the blood-stained clothes of the murderer were found at the scene, suggesting that he had changed into a fresh set of clothes before making his escape. Interestingly, despite the gruesome nature of the crime, it appeared that robbery was not the motive, as valuables and money left in plain sight were untouched. Near the crime scene, a cryptic chalk message was discovered: "Mrs. Joseph Maggio will sit up tonight. Just write Mrs. Toney." Despite several interrogations and arrests, the police were unable to find substantial evidence to hold any suspects.

The city's nightmare continued when, just over a month later, on June 27, 1918, another couple fell victim to the Axeman's relentless spree. Louis Besumer, also a grocer, and his mistress, Harriet Lowe, were found in a dreadful state, lying in a pool of their own blood at the back of Besumer's store. Besumer suffered a severe ax blow above his right temple, while Lowe was viciously hacked over her left ear. Miraculously, both were still alive when discovered. This attack sparked another wave of interrogations and arrests, but like before, no conclusive evidence was found, and all suspects were released.

The scandalous nature of Besumer and Lowe's relationship overshadowed the brutality of the attack in some public discussions. Tragically, following an operation on August 5th aimed at addressing the paralysis on one side of Lowe's face resulting from the attack, she succumbed to her injuries two days later. In her final moments, Lowe accused Besumer of being her assailant. Subsequently, Besumer was charged with murder, leading to a nine-month incarceration before being acquitted on May 1, 1919, after a jury deliberated for a mere ten minutes.

The unsettling wave of violence in New Orleans continued to escalate in the summer of 1918, with a chilling attack on August 5th, targeting Mrs. Edward Schneider, a 28-year-old woman who was eight months pregnant. This incident was not just another entry in the city's growing list of brutal assaults; it was a stark reminder of the indiscriminate nature of the menace they were facing. Mrs. Schneider, in the sanctity of her own bedroom, awoke to a nightmarish sight: a dark, ominous figure looming over her. Before she could react, she was viciously bashed in the face, an act of brutality that left her severely injured. Her husband, returning home from work just after midnight, found her in this harrowing state: her scalp viciously cut open, her face a mask of blood. Miraculously, amidst this horror, Mrs. Schneider survived and, in a testament to her resilience, gave birth to a healthy baby girl just two days later. A suspect was swiftly arrested in connection with the attack but was just as quickly released due to a lack of convincing evidence.

This attack on Mrs. Schneider prompted investigators to publicly acknowledge a potential link between this and the earlier gruesome incidents involving

Besumer, Lowe, and the Maggios. The pattern of violence against grocers and the brutality of the attacks indicated a sinister connection.

The community barely had time to process this attack before another grocer, an elderly man named Joseph Ramano, became the next victim on August 10th. This attack was horrifyingly similar to the previous ones, yet it bore its unique horrors. Ramano lived with his two nieces, who were jolted awake by the sounds of a violent struggle in their uncle's room. They rushed in only to witness a heart-stopping scene: their uncle, gravely injured with a severe head wound, and the fleeting glimpse of the assailant making a hasty escape. Despite the severity of his injuries, Ramano demonstrated a remarkable will, managing to walk to the ambulance upon its arrival. Tragically, his resilience could not overcome the brutal injuries, and he succumbed to severe head trauma two days later.

In a crucial development, Ramano's nieces provided the police with a description of the killer, a detail that had eluded the authorities in the previous attacks. They described the assailant as a dark-skinned, heavy-set man, dressed in a dark suit and a slouched hat.

The pattern of crimes attributed to the Axeman of New Orleans was not just marked by its brutality but also by its perplexing and consistent set of clues, painting a picture of a methodical and elusive perpetrator. In each of the horrifying scenes, investigators found strikingly similar patterns: homes were often left in disarray, as though ransacked, yet curiously, nothing was ever stolen. This pointed to a motive far removed from common burglary. Another chilling commonality was the killer's use of the homeowner's own tools for the ghastly deeds; hatchets and blades belonging to the victims were often found at the crime scenes. The method of entry into these homes was also a signature of sorts: panels on doors or windows meticulously chiseled away, indicating a calculated approach to gaining access to the victims. Notably, the majority of these victims shared Italian heritage, adding another layer of mystery and fear in the Italian-American communities.

This series of murders and assaults brought an overwhelming sense of terror to the city. Residents were on high alert, with the police receiving constant reports of suspicious activities. Citizens claimed to have spotted an axeman lurking in neighborhoods, finding axes and chisels in their backyards, or noticing doors and windows that appeared tampered with. The fear was palpable and led to drastic measures for self-protection. People armed themselves with loaded shotguns, and families instituted night watches, taking turns to vigilantly guard their loved ones. Rumors and speculations ran rampant, with one report suggesting the Axeman was disguising himself as a woman, while another claimed he was seen leaping over a backyard fence.

The city was gripped by a mix of fear and determination, teetering on the edge of panic. However, as if in response to the intense scrutiny and terror, the killings and assaults mysteriously ceased as abruptly as they had begun. This sudden halt provided a temporary respite, but the shadow of the Axeman still loomed large over the city.

This sense of normalcy was shattered on March 10, 1919, when the Axeman reemerged with another heinous attack. This time, the victim was Charles Cortimiglia, an immigrant and grocer residing with his wife, Rosie, and their two-year-old daughter, Mary, in Gretna, a town just across the Mississippi River from New Orleans. In the early hours, the neighborhood was pierced by screams emanating from the Cortimiglia residence. Alarmed, Lorlando Jordano, a neighboring grocer, rushed to the scene to find a sight of pure horror: the Cortimiglia family had been savagely attacked. This incident reignited the fear and uncertainty in the hearts of the New Orleans residents, reminding them that the terror of the Axeman was far from over.

Rosie Cortimiglia, awoken by the commotion, witnessed a nightmarish scene: her husband, Charles, engaged in a desperate struggle with a large, axe-wielding man. As Charles fell to the floor, defeated, the assailant turned his murderous intent towards Rosie, who clutched their daughter, pleading for mercy. Her pleas fell on deaf ears; the assailant mercilessly attacked both mother and child with the axe.

When their neighbor, Lorlando Jordano, arrived at the Cortimiglia residence, the scene was one of sheer horror. Charles lay in a pool of his own blood, while Rosie, despite a serious head wound, stood in the doorway holding the lifeless body of their daughter. The couple was quickly rushed to the hospital. Charles, though severely injured, was released after two days, but Rosie's injuries were more critical, necessitating prolonged medical care.

In a shocking twist, upon regaining full consciousness, Rosie accused their neighbor and fellow grocer, Lorlando Jordano, and his 18-year-old son, Frank, of the brutal attack. This accusation seemed implausible; Lorlando, at 69 years of age, was in frail health, unlikely to commit such a physically demanding crime, and Frank's large build made it improbable for him to fit through the chiseled panel of the back door used by the attacker. Nevertheless, the Jordano father and son were arrested. Despite Charles Cortimiglia's denial of his wife's accusations, the Jordanos were charged and subsequently found guilty. Frank received a death sentence, while his father was sentenced to life in prison. The case took an even more dramatic turn when Charles, in the aftermath of the trial, divorced Rosie.

About a year later, in a startling confession, Rosie reversed her claim, admitting that she had falsely accused the Jordanos out of jealousy and spite. This admission, considering her testimony was the only evidence against them, led to the release of both Lorlando and Frank Jordano from prison.

Following the Cortimiglia incident, the city of New Orleans once again found itself engulfed in fear. Citizens armed themselves, vigilant against the threat of the Axeman. The police, grappling with the escalating panic and a series of unsolved brutal crimes, described the perpetrator as "a bloodthirsty maniac, filled with a passion for human slaughter." This description only served to heighten the sense of terror among the residents, who were left wondering who would be next in the Axeman's path of destruction.

In March 1919, the city of New Orleans was further plunged into fear and confusion by a bizarre and sinister twist in the ongoing Axeman saga. The Times-Picayune newspaper received a letter, chillingly dated "Hell, March 13, 1919," and purportedly from the Axeman himself. This letter was both taunting and terrifying in its content, adding a surreal aspect to the already tense atmosphere in the city.

The letter claimed that the Axeman was not a human but a demonic spirit, invisible and all-powerful, mocking the futile attempts by the police to capture him. He boasted of his invisibility and his connection with the supernatural, specifically aligning himself with the 'Angel of Death' and implying his invulnerability to human efforts of capture or restraint.

Most bizarrely, the letter contained a peculiar demand intertwined with a grim threat. The Axeman declared his fondness for jazz music and made a macabre offer: on a specified date and time, any household playing jazz music would be spared his wrath. The implication was clear and terrifying – those not heeding his demand and playing jazz at the appointed time risked becoming his next victims.

This letter not only heightened the existing fear among the residents but also added a layer of the surreal to the entire ordeal. The peculiar demand for jazz music turned households into bizarre scenes of forced merriment, as residents desperately sought to protect themselves from the Axeman's threatened return. The Axeman's correspondence transformed him in the public's imagination from a mere mortal criminal into a sinister, almost supernatural figure, terrorizing the city with his unpredictable and incomprehensible whims.

In response to the Axeman's chilling letter, the people of New Orleans took no chances on the night of March 19, 1919. Homes across the city resonated with the lively sounds of jazz, as residents heeded the killer's bizarre demand. Dance halls were packed, and jazz music emanated from parties in hundreds of houses, creating an almost surreal atmosphere of forced festivity underpinned by a palpable sense of fear. That night, amidst this citywide embrace of jazz, there were no reports of attacks, seemingly affirming the Axeman's ominous promise.

However, the respite was short-lived, and the underlying tension remained. Weeks of quiet passed, but the fear lingered like a dark cloud over the city. Then, on August 10, 1919, the Axeman struck again. Steve Boca, another grocer, became the latest victim in this string of brutal attacks. Boca was assaulted in his bedroom, waking up to the terrifying sight of a dark figure standing over him. Suffering a severe blow from an axe, he managed to escape and seek help from his neighbor, Frank Genusa, before losing consciousness. Miraculously, he survived, but like the other victims, he couldn't recall the details of the attack. The crime scene bore the Axeman's signature - nothing stolen and a chiseled panel on the back door.

The Axeman's reign of terror continued. On September 2, local druggist William Carson had a narrow escape when he fired shots at an intruder, presumably the Axeman, who broke into his home, leaving behind a broken door and an axe. The very next day, on September 3, 1919, a young girl named Sarah Laumann became the next target. Neighbors found her unconscious in her locked and shuttered home, suffering from a severe head wound and missing teeth. A bloody axe was discovered on the front lawn, adding to the eerie pattern of attacks.

New Orleans was again in hysteria when, after two months of calm, grocer Mike Pepitone was brutally murdered in his home on October 27, 1919. His wife witnessed a large man with an axe fleeing the scene. Pepitone, left fatally wounded and leaving behind a wife and six children, was the Axeman's final known victim. Despite no description of the assailant and the authorities' efforts, the case went unsolved. The Axeman's identity and motives remained unknown, casting a lasting shadow of fear and mystery over New Orleans.

Hinterkaifeck Murders

In the early spring of April 1922, a harrowing and mysterious event unfolded at Hinterkaifeck, a secluded farm nestled amidst the dense forests between two Bavarian towns, roughly 70 kilometers north of Munich. This small farmstead, shrouded in an eerie silence, became the scene of a gruesome discovery. The Gruber family, consisting of Andreas and Cazilia, aged 63 and 72 respectively, their widowed daughter Viktoria, 35, and her two young children, 7-year-old Cazilia and 2-year-old Josef, along with a maid, were found brutally murdered. The method of their demise was chilling – they had been bludgeoned to death.

What added to the macabre nature of the crime was the revelation that the family had been deceased for several days before their bodies were discovered. Yet, witnesses reported seeing signs of life within the farmhouse just a day prior to the discovery. This eerie detail led to a horrifying conclusion: the perpetrator, or perpetrators, had continued living on the farm, amidst the lifeless bodies of the Gruber family, for almost a week.

The case was shrouded in mystery and darkness. Many questioned if there were premonitions or ominous signs in the months leading up to the tragic event. Rumors and whispers of the farm being haunted circulated among the locals, fueling a sense of unease and superstition. The question also arose whether the killer was someone from within the community, perhaps even someone known to the family.

The Grubers, despite their seemingly ordinary life as farmers, were not without scandal. They were viewed with suspicion and disdain by their neighbors, primarily due to the scandalous and criminal nature of Viktoria and Andreas' relationship. Accusations and eventual convictions of incest had marred their reputation, with many believing that Josef was a product of this illicit union. Andreas served a year in prison for the crime, while Viktoria spent a month behind bars.

Their notorious reputation led the Grubers to live a reclusive life, with only Viktoria and young Cazilia being occasionally seen in town. This isolation meant that their absence went largely unnoticed; few in the surrounding communities would find it unusual or alarming if the family wasn't seen for several days. This social isolation, combined with the farm's remote location, created a perfect storm of circumstances, allowing a heinous crime to go undetected for days.

The family's maid, who had been a part of the household for some time, abruptly resigned her position. Her departure was shrouded in whispers and rumors, as she claimed that the farm was haunted. Her accounts to the local police were laced with fear and apprehension, detailing eerie occurrences that would chill the bones of even the most skeptical listener.

According to her testimony, the maid was tormented by unexplainable phenomena. She spoke of hearing the unsettling sound of footsteps in the dead of night, emanating from the vacant attic above. These nocturnal disturbances, she insisted, were not the work of living beings. While many reports circulated about her claims, the most striking part of her police interview was her assertion that every night at the stroke of midnight, the door would eerily swing open on its own. Whatever the truth of her experiences, the terror she felt was palpable, compelling her to flee the farmstead in search of peace and safety.

Andreas Gruber, the patriarch of the family, outwardly dismissed these claims as fanciful tales. He shared with neighbors his skepticism about the alleged haunting. However, as autumn gave way to the bitter chill of winter, Andreas himself began to experience these unexplained disturbances. His nights were disrupted by the same peculiar sounds that had driven the maid away. Determined to uncover the source, Andreas conducted a thorough investigation of the property but found nothing that could explain the mysterious noises. Despite his initial bravado, the unanswered questions lingered, creating an undercurrent of unease that even he could not ignore.

As March 1922 approached, bringing with it the harshness of a late-season snowstorm, the farmstead found itself blanketed in a pristine layer of snow. It was during this time that Andreas stumbled upon a chilling discovery that would further deepen the mystery surrounding Hinterkaifeck. Emerging from the depths of the forest and leading directly to the farm's machine room were a set of lone footprints. The lock on the machine room, broken for several weeks, had not been repaired, fueling speculation that someone had been using it as a shelter.

Andreas' search of the machine room and other areas of the farm yielded no answers, only deepening the enigma. The absence of any footprints leading back to the forest left him with a sense of foreboding, a feeling that something or someone unseen was lurking nearby.

In the days that followed, more odd occurrences unfolded. Andreas discovered a newspaper on the property that no one in the family claimed to have bought. In those times, newspapers were either subscribed to or bought in town, yet this particular publication was unfamiliar to both the Grubers and their neighbors.

The local community began to whisper about the Grubers' misfortunes, with neighbors recounting stories of the family mentioning missing house keys and frequent sightings of a mysterious stranger with a mustache prowling the outskirts of the farm.

The unsettling atmosphere reached its peak on Friday, March 31st, 1922, when 44-year-old Maria Baumgartner arrived at Hinterkaifeck to begin her tenure as the new maid. Little did she know that her first day on the job would also mark the beginning of a tragic chapter in the annals of unsolved crimes.

As the first week of April 1922 unfolded, an eerie quiet had settled over the Hinterkaifeck farmstead, a silence that was about to be shattered by a series of unsettling observations and discoveries. The Gruber family, usually a common sight in their daily routines, had strangely not been seen by anyone for several days. Yet, there were fleeting glimpses of activity at the farm that, unbeknownst to the onlookers, were not the doings of the family.

On the evening of April 1st, a local artisan named Michel Plockl passed by the farm and noticed something peculiar. Smoke was billowing from the chimney, a usual sign of life, but on this occasion, it seemed oddly out of place. He also spotted a figure outside, illuminated by the faint glow of a lantern. However, the distance and dim light made it impossible for him to identify who it was.

The following night added to the growing sense of unease. Simon Reiblander, a farmer and butcher by trade, observed two strangers near the edge of the forest bordering the Gruber property. As he moved closer, hoping to discern their identity, the figures abruptly turned and vanished into the sheltering darkness of the trees.

By April 3rd, these strange occurrences had begun to arouse suspicion. The local postman, making his regular rounds, was struck by an odd detail: the mail he had delivered on Saturday remained untouched. This was highly unusual for the typically prompt Gruber family.

The situation grew more curious on April 4th. That day, repairman Albert Hofner arrived at the farmstead with a task to complete: fixing an engine in the farm's machine room. As he approached, the absence of the family was palpable. The barn doors were securely locked, and from within, he could hear the family's dog barking incessantly.

Albert, absorbed in his work, paid little attention to these peculiarities. He entered the open machine room and set about his task, oblivious to the sinister undercurrents swirling around him. It took him four hours to complete the repair, and upon exiting the farmstead, he was greeted by a scene that chilled him to the bone. The previously locked barn door now stood ajar, and the dog, which had been locked inside, was now tied up outside. This was peculiar, as he hadn't seen or heard any sign of the family throughout his time there.

Troubled by what he had witnessed, Albert returned to the town and recounted his eerie experience to Lorenz Schlittenbauer, a local guide and acquaintance of the Grubers. Lorenz, already concerned by the family's uncharacteristic disappearance, was spurred into action by Albert's account. Deciding that something was amiss, he gathered two of his friends and, with a sense of foreboding, set out for the Hinterkaifeck farm at around 3:30 pm, unaware that they were about to stumble upon a scene that would forever be etched in the annals of true crime history.

On that fateful day, as the sun began its descent in the Bavarian sky, three men, led by Lorenz Schlittenbauer, approached the eerily quiet Hinterkaifeck farmstead with a growing sense of trepidation. The air was heavy with an unspoken dread as they arrived at the house, only to find every door stubbornly locked, the windows offering no glimpse into the mysteries within. A palpable sense of unease hung over the property, as if the very walls were holding their breath.

Their attention was drawn to the barn, where the door hung open, an unspoken invitation into the unknown. With hesitant steps, they entered the shadowy interior. The sight that met their eyes was one of unimaginable horror: the lifeless bodies of Andreas Gruber, his wife Cazilia, their daughter Viktoria, and their young granddaughter Cazilia were piled atop one another, unceremoniously covered in hay as if to hide the brutality of their end.

Lorenz, driven by a faint hope that some life might remain, moved each body in a desperate search for signs of life. The grim reality quickly set in; they were all beyond help. Panic surged through him as he realized that young Josef, the toddler of the household, was not among the bodies. With a sense of urgency, he dashed through a connecting hallway from the barn into the house, his heart pounding with fear and dread.

Inside the house, a scene of equal horror unfolded. There, he found the bloodied body of Maria Baumgartner, the new maid whose first day had tragically become her last. Nearby, in a haunting tableau of innocence lost, lay the small, still form of Josef, resting in his bassinet, a silent witness to the unspeakable tragedy that had befallen his family.

Hours passed before Inspector Georg Reingruber of the Munich Police Department could arrive at the scene. The remote location of the farm meant a grueling 45-mile journey, a distance that in those days seemed much further than it does now. In the small community, news, particularly of a tragedy as shocking as a multiple murder, traveled with alarming speed, outpacing the law's ability to respond.

By the time the authorities arrived, the crime scene had been compromised. Reports from the time tell of townsfolk, drawn by a macabre curiosity, trampling around the scene, heedlessly moving evidence, their actions driven by a mixture of fear, intrigue, and disbelief. In a disturbing display of insensitivity, some even cooked and ate meals within the walls of the crime scene, oblivious or indifferent to the sanctity of the space they had invaded.

The following day, an autopsy was conducted, revealing the brutal manner in which the family had met their end. Each victim had been struck with a mattock, a tool akin to a pickaxe, with merciless force. The autopsy revealed a detail even more harrowing: the younger Cazilia had not died instantly like the others. Instead, she had lingered for hours after the attack, the shock and trauma of witnessing her family's murder driving her to a state of unimaginable distress, evidenced by clumps of her own hair found clenched in her lifeless hands – a silent testament to her final, agonizing moments.

The macabre puzzle of the Hinterkaifeck murders presented the police with a complex and chilling challenge. As they delved deeper into the investigation, piecing together the fragments of evidence and accounts from various interviews, a sinister timeline began to emerge, shedding light on the events leading up to that fateful night.

A crucial piece of this puzzle was an interview with the sister of Maria Baumgartner, the new maid whose first day tragically coincided with the massacre. She confirmed that she had visited Maria on March 31st, establishing that day as Maria's first and only day at the farm. This detail, combined with the testimony of the local mailman, who noted that the mail had remained undisturbed since the morning of Saturday, April 1st, led the police to a grim conclusion: the brutal murders likely occurred on the night of March 31st.

The investigators speculated that on that ill-fated night, the killer or killers had used some cunning means to lure each member of the Gruber family into the barn, one by one. Perhaps through deceptive calls or by creating a disturbance, they drew the unsuspecting victims into the darkness. There, in the secluded confines of the barn, each family member was mercilessly attacked with a pickaxe, struck repeatedly in the head. Viktoria and her mother Cazilia bore additional signs of a struggle, suggesting they might have been strangled before also succumbing to the fatal blows of the pickaxe.

Viktoria, in a particularly brutal display of violence, had been struck multiple times, receiving upwards of nine blows. The assailant then moved into the house, where Maria Baumgartner met her tragic end in her room. The final act of this gruesome drama was the killing of little Josef, who was struck just once, a blow that ended his life instantly.

As the investigation continued, interviews with neighbors and a thorough examination of the scene revealed an even more disturbing aspect of the killer's behavior. In the days following the murders, some locals reported seeing smoke rising from the chimney of the Gruber home, leading to speculation that someone was still inside. Some even believed they had glimpsed one of the Gruber family members outside the house.

Further adding to the eerie nature of the case, the police found evidence that someone had been tending to the daily chores on the farm. The dog and cattle had been fed, the cows milked, and food prepared and cooked. This chilling realization suggested that the murderer or murderers not only committed the heinous acts but also callously continued to live on the farm for several days afterward, demonstrating a familiarity with the property and its routines.

The interview with Albert Hofner, the repairman who visited the farm on the day the bodies were discovered, provided another unnerving detail. The police deduced that the killers might have been present in the house even as Albert worked on the farm machinery, unseen and undetected. This raised a haunting question: had the murderers still been on the property when the police arrived? Were they hiding in plain sight, masquerading as grieving neighbors?

As the investigation into the grisly Hinterkaifeck murders unfolded, the police began to consider various theories to unravel the mystery. One of the earliest hypotheses they explored was the possibility of a robbery gone awry. This line of inquiry was partly fueled by an intriguing interview with Kreszenz Rieger, who had previously worked as a maid for the Gruber family.

Kreszenz recounted a particularly suspicious encounter that occurred almost a year before the murders. She described a visit to the farm by a man named Josef Thaler, who, along with his brother, was known in the local area for their involvement in various minor burglaries. One eerie night, Josef had tapped on Kreszenz's window, persistently trying to gain her attention. When she finally responded, Josef insinuated a sinister interest in the farm, probing

Kreszenz for information about where the family slept.

Kreszenz, wary of Josef's intentions, refused to divulge any details and feigned ignorance. As they conversed, she noticed another figure lurking in the bushes behind Josef, whom he claimed was not there. However, she was convinced that he was accompanied by his brother, especially when she later saw them both near the barn, their gaze ominously fixed on the roof.

Adding to the police's suspicions, Kreszenz revealed a past incident where the Thaler brothers had hidden in the Grubers' barn. Andreas Gruber had discovered them and reportedly fired shots towards them with a rifle to chase them away.

While the Thaler brothers initially appeared to be strong suspects, this theory was weakened by the fact that valuables such as money, gold, and jewelry were found untouched in the Grubers' home after the murders. This indicated that the motive behind the killings was something other than robbery.

Several days into the investigation, Inspector Reingruber shifted his focus to another suspect: Adolf Gump. Rumors had circulated about Adolf having been romantically involved with Viktoria Gruber. However, the evidence linking him to the family or placing him at the scene of the crime was tenuous at best. Adolf had previously been suspected, alongside three others, of involvement in the killing of nine peasants in 1921, but this alone was hardly conclusive.

Adolf Gump remained elusive and was never interrogated, as he could not be located by the police.

The case took a dramatic turn thirty years later, in 1951, when a deathbed confession by Adolf's sister, Kreszentia Mayer, brought new attention to the long-cold case. She claimed that her brothers, Adolf and Anton Gump, were responsible for the Hinterkaifeck murders. In light of this revelation, prosecutor Andreas Popp detained Anton Gump for questioning. However,

Adolf was beyond the reach of justice, having died in 1944 during the Second World War.

Despite the gravity of Kreszentia's confession, the lack of concrete evidence against the Gump brothers and Anton's steadfast claims of innocence led to his eventual release. By 1954, the case against Anton was formally dropped, leaving the haunting mystery of the Hinterkaifeck murders unsolved.

Another suspect was Karl Gabriel, the deceased husband of Viktoria, the widowed daughter of the Gruber family. This line of inquiry was sparked by the peculiar circumstances surrounding Karl's supposed death.

Karl Gabriel was believed to have fallen in battle in France in December 1914, during the tumultuous days of the First World War. However, the fact that his body was never recovered ignited a flicker of doubt and gave birth to one of the more unconventional theories regarding the Hinterkaifeck murders. In the absence of physical evidence of his death, some began to speculate that perhaps Karl had not perished in the war after all.

As the investigation hit dead ends and the pressure to find the killer mounted, people began to entertain the possibility that Karl had miraculously returned to the farm, only to discover the existence of Viktoria's son, Josef. This revelation, they theorized, might have triggered a rage in Karl, whether due to suspicions of an incestuous liaison between Viktoria and Andreas, or simply the betrayal of Viktoria having a child with another man. According to this theory, it was Karl who, in a fit of vengeful fury, annihilated the entire family.

In a move that seemed almost desperate, the police even considered this theory seriously. Fuel was added to the speculative fire by numerous individuals who, in the years following the murders, claimed to have seen a man resembling Karl Gabriel in the vicinity, both during and after the time of the killings.

However, the police's thorough investigation, which included interviews with

Karl's fellow soldiers, eventually confirmed that he had indeed died in the war. Multiple eyewitness accounts attested to seeing Karl lifeless following a shell attack in France. Despite this confirmation, the mystery and intrigue surrounding Karl Gabriel's supposed involvement in the murders persisted in various articles and discussions, keeping his name alive as a potential suspect in one of the most baffling and haunting unsolved crimes of the 20th century.

While numerous individuals have been postulated as potential culprits over the years, many of these theories lack substantial evidence. However, one suspect who stands out, both for his close ties to the family and the peculiarities surrounding his actions, is Lorenz Schlittenbauer, the town's tour guide and the man who discovered the bodies.

Lorenz's involvement in the case is not merely limited to his discovery of the gruesome scene. His actions and connections to the Gruber family cast a shadow of suspicion over him, making him a figure of significant interest in this enduring mystery. His behavior at the crime scene, particularly his handling of the bodies and his seemingly composed demeanor, raised eyebrows. In an era where forensic science was in its infancy, it was commonly understood that a crime scene should be left untouched. Yet, Lorenz seemed to disregard this principle, moving the bodies and even entering the house alone – actions that many deemed highly irregular.

Adding to the suspicion was the observation by some witnesses that Lorenz's reactions upon discovering the bloodied corpses were unusually calm, lacking any visible signs of horror or revulsion. Rumors swirled around the town that Lorenz had in his possession a key to the Gruber's house, echoing back to Andreas Gruber's report of missing keys prior to his tragic death.

When questioned by the authorities, Lorenz offered an explanation that only deepened the mystery. He confessed to a rumor that had been circulating in the community – that he was the biological father of young Josef. Lorenz justified his actions at the crime scene by stating that he was desperately searching for his son amidst the carnage. This claim, however, conflicted with his previous denials of paternity, which he explained away by citing the incest allegations between Viktoria and Andreas Gruber that had cast doubt on his mind about the child's parentage.

This tangled web of relationships and accusations took a more sinister turn when the police uncovered legal records indicating that Viktoria had sought court-mandated alimony payments from Lorenz. This revelation lent credence to the theory that Lorenz, already burdened by financial troubles and responsibilities to another family, might have had a motive to commit the murders – to escape the financial burden of the alimony payments.

Witness accounts further complicated the narrative. Several people claimed to have seen Lorenz and Viktoria engaged in heated arguments over the alimony and the paternity of Josef, with some stating these confrontations occurred as recently as on the day of the murders.

Another twist in the tale emerged with suggestions that Lorenz, who initially doubted his paternity, later claimed to be Josef's father in a bid to lay claim to a potential inheritance from the Gruber family.

The haunting tale of the Hinterkaifeck murders, shrouded in mystery and speculation, remains one of the most perplexing cold cases in criminal history. Despite the myriad of theories and allegations that surfaced over the years, they ultimately remained just that - theories, unsubstantiated by concrete evidence. This lack of definitive proof stymied the police's efforts to solve the case, leaving a void filled with unanswered questions and enduring intrigue.

Lorenz Schlittenbauer, a central figure in the web of suspicion, defended his actions at the crime scene by claiming a single-minded focus on finding his son amidst the horror. His apparent lack of emotional response to the gruesome scene was attributed by some to shock, a not uncommon reaction in the face of such overwhelming and brutal tragedy. Without substantial evidence to the contrary, the police found no grounds to arrest him. Lorenz's name was often whispered in connection with the crime, but he staunchly defended his innocence, successfully contesting numerous accusations of slander in court until his death in 1941.

Over the years, the police cast a wide net in their search for the perpetrator, suspecting as many as one hundred individuals, yet not a single arrest was made, nor charges brought forward. The official investigation was eventually closed in 1955, but the enigmatic nature of the case ensured it lingered in the collective memory, a haunting reminder of justice unfulfilled.

In a modern twist, the case was revisited in 2007 by a group of students from a German police academy, who applied contemporary forensic techniques in their examination of the available evidence. While they acknowledged the near impossibility of solving the crime after so many decades, their analysis led them to identify a prime suspect. However, out of respect for the descendants of the suspect, they chose to keep the identity confidential.

Now, a century after the tragic events at Hinterkaifeck, the likelihood of unraveling the truth grows ever more remote. Yet, the story continues to captivate and inspire new generations of amateur sleuths and professional investigators alike, all driven by the hope of bringing closure to a case that has long haunted the annals of unsolved crimes.

At the heart of this enduring mystery is the undeniable tragedy of six lives brutally and senselessly extinguished. The Hinterkaifeck murders stand as a stark reminder of the capacity for evil and hatred that can manifest in the human heart, leaving behind a legacy of sorrow and an unquenchable yearning for justice in the face of an unspeakable crime.

Murder of Peter Porco

On a quiet autumn morning, November 15, 2004, the small town of Delmar, New York, was shaken by a gruesome discovery. Peter Porco, a 52-year-old respected clerk at the state Appellate Division, was found lifeless in his home, succumbing to horrific head injuries. The scene at the Porco residence was one of unimaginable horror: bloodstains painted the walls and floors, telling a silent tale of violence and desperation.

Peter's wife, Joan Porco (née Balzano), known in the community as a compassionate children's speech pathologist, lay in their bed, barely clinging to life. She had suffered appalling head trauma, resulting in the loss of an eye, part of her skull, and severe facial disfigurement. Miraculously, she survived the attack, but her life was irrevocably changed.

In a bizarre twist, despite Peter's catastrophic injuries, he managed to survive for several hours post-attack. In a state of confusion and agony, he attempted to carry on with his morning routine, unaware of the gravity of his condition. He wrote a check for his son Christopher, prepared a packed lunch, and even tried to load the dishwasher – mundane tasks that stood in stark contrast to the brutal reality of his final moments.

The weapon, an axe belonging to the family, was later discovered in the garage, a silent witness to the atrocity. The Bethlehem Police Department, tasked with unraveling this macabre puzzle, quickly turned their attention to Christopher Porco, the younger of Peter and Joan's two sons. At the time of the attack, Christopher was a university student at the University of Rochester, approximately 230 miles away from the crime scene.

Christopher maintained that he was at the university when his parents were discovered in their blood-soaked home. He claimed to have first heard about the attack from a reporter, a statement that raised more questions than answers. He returned to Delmar the same evening, stepping into a maelstrom of suspicion and inquiry.

As the investigation deepened, outgoing Albany County District Attorney Paul Clyne took a decisive step in late November 2004. He convened a grand jury to hear testimony that might implicate Christopher in the heinous crime. The closed-session hearing drew in various figures from Christopher's life, including friends from college, a university campus safety officer, and a former girlfriend. Their testimonies were critical pieces in a complex and disturbing puzzle.

The grand jury's work continued, delving deeper into the details and circumstances surrounding the tragic event. Finally, in November 2005, a full year after the brutal attacks, an indictment was handed up against Christopher Porco, setting the stage for a trial that would captivate and horrify the public. This case, rooted in a small town, would soon capture the attention of a nation, as layers of tragedy, mystery, and familial betrayal were slowly unraveled.

In the intricate investigation, authorities uncovered a pattern of Christopher's troubling behavior. One significant incident involved a burglary at his parents' home. In a bold and calculated move, Christopher had stolen a laptop from his own home in July 2003 and later sold it on eBay. This incident was not an isolated one; it was revealed that in November 2002, Christopher staged another burglary at his parents' house. During this incident, he took not one, but two laptop computers – a Macintosh and a Dell – and a camera, which was later found abandoned in the front yard. These brazen acts of theft from his own family were just the tip of the iceberg.

The situation escalated when Christopher and his brother Johnathan's eBay accounts were frozen due to their shared address. Christopher had failed to deliver items to several customers. In a desperate attempt to cover his tracks, he posed as his brother in emails, deceitfully claiming that Johnathan had passed away and hence could not fulfill the orders. This disturbing behavior hinted at a deeper, more sinister aspect of Christopher's character.

The events of November 15, 2004, brought these underlying issues to a head. On that fateful day, the Porco family's security system was disabled using their own code, followed by the severing of the telephone line outside their home. Prosecutors argued that Christopher was responsible for these acts, aiming to stage the crime scene as a burglary.

Amidst these criminal activities, Christopher's academic and financial struggles came to light. In March 2004, while Christopher was in England, his parents confronted him about his failing grades at Hudson Valley Community College. Their disappointment was evident in an email with a subject header that read "Failing Grades-You did it again!" Christopher's response attempted to deflect blame onto the college's registrar, claiming inaccuracies in his reported grades. However, his academic struggles were real, as he had been forced to withdraw from the University of Rochester due to poor performance. In a desperate attempt to return to university, Christopher forged a transcript from Hudson Valley Community College.

Financial tensions further strained Christopher's relationship with his parents. He had taken substantial loans, not only for tuition but also for a Jeep Wrangler. To compound matters, he deceitfully used a $31,000 loan, forged in his father's name, to pay his university expenses, all while misleading his parents about the source of his tuition funding.

In the weeks leading up to the tragic murder of Peter Porco, a troubling email exchange between him and his son Christopher revealed deep family tensions and a father's growing concern over his son's deceitful actions. The gravity of the situation was clear: Peter had discovered Christopher's forgery of his signature to secure a loan. In a stern yet bewildered tone, Peter wrote to Christopher, questioning his actions and expressing his deep disappointment: "Did you forge my signature as a co-signer? ... What the hell are you doing? You should have called me to discuss it ..."

Determined to address the issue, Peter informed Christopher of his intent to contact Citibank to clarify the situation. The revelation of Christopher's deception was not limited to this instance. The following day, Peter discovered that Christopher had also obtained a line of credit from Citibank to finance a Jeep Wrangler, again fraudulently using his father's name. This prompted another email from Peter, who had been unable to reach Christopher by phone for weeks. In this email, Peter conveyed a stern warning about the consequences of further misuse of his credit, including the possibility of filing forgery affidavits.

Despite the severity of the situation, Peter's email ended on a note of parental love and concern, highlighting the complex emotions involved: "We may be disappointed with you, but your mother and I still love you and care about your future." This poignant conclusion underscored the heartbreak and conflict inherent in the family's ordeal.

The trial brought further insights into the Porco family dynamics, particularly through the testimony of Christopher's brother, Johnathan. As reported by the Albany Times Union, Johnathan's testimony was pivotal, characterized by a cold and distant demeanor towards his brother. He described their relationship as "strained," painting a picture of a fractured family struggling with internal conflicts.

The police, in their investigation, posited that Christopher Porco's actions were indicative of psychopathy or sociopathy, disorders marked by a pattern of deceitful behavior, lack of remorse, and the manipulation of others for personal gain. Christopher's life was a facade of lies, from securing funds for a car and tuition to fabricating stories about his family's wealth and lifestyle.

This perspective was further explored by Professor Frank Perri, who critiqued the police interviews with Christopher Porco. He argued that the investigative approach was flawed, failing to adequately consider Christopher's probable psychopathy. This oversight, Perri suggested, might have influenced the effectiveness of the police questioning, potentially impacting the investigation's trajectory.

Christopher maintained to investigators that on the night of November 14, he had simply slept in a dormitory lounge at the University of Rochester and woke up the following morning, seemingly uninvolved in the incident. However, the police developed a contrasting theory. They believed Christopher had driven over three hours from Rochester to Albany in the early hours of November 15 to carry out the attack on his parents. This theory was bolstered by the testimony of a New York State Thruway toll collector who vividly remembered a yellow Jeep Wrangler, resembling Christopher's, passing through his station near Rochester at around 10:45 p.m. on November 14. Similarly, a toll collector in Albany recalled the same vehicle, noting its excessive speed as it approached the toll plaza just before 2 a.m. on November 15.

The intrigue deepened with the revelation of security footage from the University of Rochester. Four cameras had captured a yellow Jeep Wrangler, identical to Christopher's, leaving the campus at 10:30 p.m. on November 14 and returning at 8:30 a.m. the next day. This timing was crucial, as it coincided with the period the prosecution claimed the Porcos were attacked.

Adding to the mounting evidence, a neighbor of the Porco family testified during the trial that he had seen Porco's distinctive yellow Jeep in the family's driveway on the evening of the attack. Furthermore, Christopher's alibi was contradicted by fellow University of Rochester students who testified they did not see him sleeping in the dormitory lounge on the night in question.

Another compelling piece of testimony came from Christopher's employer, veterinarian John Kearney. He mentioned that Christopher had been trained in cleaning up after animal surgeries, a skill that jurors later noted could explain the absence of blood in Porco's vehicle following the attack.

A dramatic moment in the investigation occurred when Bethlehem Police detective Christopher Bowdish, while medical personnel attended to Joan Porco at her home, asked her if she could identify her attacker. According to Bowdish, Joan indicated with her head movements that a family member was responsible, negating the possibility of her older son Johnathan, and instead seemingly implicating Christopher.

However, the case took a startling turn when Joan Porco, after emerging from a medically induced coma, claimed to have no memory of the attack and steadfastly maintained her belief in Christopher's innocence. This was a stark contrast to her earlier non-verbal indications to Detective Bowdish. In December 2004, during a videotaped testimony for the grand jury, Joan spoke about her family but did not identify Christopher as the attacker. Nine months later, she penned a heartfelt letter to the Albany Times Union, imploring authorities to seek the real perpetrator of the crime, a plea that highlighted the complex and emotional layers of the case.

The defense strategy in the trial of Christopher Porco was characterized by a strong emphasis on the lack of direct physical evidence and a critique of the investigative methods employed by the Bethlehem Police Department. Terence Kindlon, Porco's defense attorney, highlighted the absence of Christopher's fingerprints on the axe found at the crime scene, an axe that had been stored in the Porco's garage, thereby questioning the prosecution's narrative linking Christopher to the brutal attack on his parents.

In various statements to the press and during the criminal proceedings, Kindlon suggested that the Bethlehem Police Department had prematurely and unjustly zeroed in on Christopher as the prime suspect. Kindlon painted a picture of an inexperienced police department, more accustomed to minor disturbances than serious crime investigations, during his opening remarks to jurors on June 27, 2006. He juxtaposed the local police's typical activities, such as dealing with skateboarders at a convenience store, with the gravity and complexity of a murder investigation, implying a lack of requisite expertise for such a high-profile case.

Adding another layer to the defense's argument, Laurie Shanks, Kindlon's co-counsel and wife, proposed an alternative theory involving Peter Porco's uncle, Frank Porco, a captain in the Bonanno crime family. Shanks suggested that Peter's death might have been related to Frank's criminal activities, despite the fact that the police had already pursued and dismissed this lead. She brought attention to Frank's mob nickname, "The Fireman", and speculated on its possible connection to the murder weapon, an axe, which Peter and Joan had referred to as a "fire axe".

The trial, which began on June 27, 2006, was moved to Orange County due to the intense media coverage in the Albany area and the recusal of Albany County judges, given Peter Porco's position as a law clerk in the Courthouse.

After the prosecution presented its case against Christopher Porco, the defense's presentation was notably shorter. The jury began deliberations on the morning of August 10, 2006, and later that day, Porco was found guilty of second-degree murder and attempted murder.

On December 12, 2006, Judge Jeffrey Berry, expressing concern about the possibility of a similar incident occurring again, sentenced Porco to 50 years to life on each count, amounting to a minimum of 50 years in prison. Porco will be eligible for parole in December 2052.

Incarcerated at Clinton Correctional Facility, Christopher Porco's subsequent appeals to the Appellate Division, Third Department, the New York Court of Appeals, and the U.S. Supreme Court were all unsuccessful.

The Porco case has captured public attention through various media portrayals, including episodes of "Forensic Files", "Great Crimes and Trials", and CBS's "48 Hours". Additionally, Lifetime aired a movie titled "Romeo Killer: The Chris Porco Story" in 2013, against which Porco filed an unsuccessful lawsuit to block its release.

In a recent development, on January 12, 2023, WTEN reporter John Gray interviewed Christopher Porco in prison. During the interview, which aired on News 10 ABC, Porco claimed to have filed a motion for ineffective counsel, citing a misplaced paper he alleges would prove his alibi. The current status of this motion remains unknown, adding yet another chapter to the complex and ongoing narrative of the Porco case.

Panmunjom Axe Murders

In the tense and politically charged atmosphere of the Korean Demilitarized Zone (DMZ), a unique incident unfolded that would later be known as the "Axe Murder Incident." This event occurred in the Joint Security Area (JSA), a neutral zone where North Korean and South Korean forces stand face to face. At the heart of this area, near the iconic Bridge of No Return, which marks the Military Demarcation Line, a significant symbol of division and conflict loomed: a 30-meter tall poplar tree. This tree was not just a natural feature; it became a point of contention due to its location, as it obstructed the line of sight between a United Nations Command (UNC) checkpoint and an observation post.

The tree's strategic significance was highlighted in a tense encounter prior to the infamous incident. North Korean soldiers, asserting their presence and power, once detained a group of US troops at gunpoint in this very area. This alarming situation led to the deployment of Joint Security Force (JSF) company commander Captain Arthur Bonifas. His mission was clear and perilous: to confront the North Koreans, deescalate the standoff, and ensure the safe return of the American soldiers. Captain Bonifas executed this task with commendable bravery and tactical acumen, successfully bringing the troops back to safety. However, this wouldn't be the last of the confrontations involving Captain Bonifas in this volatile region.

The poplar tree's significance was further amplified by a claim from the North Korean side. Wayne Kirkbride, an officer stationed at the DMZ during this period, recounted an intriguing detail that added a layer of complexity to the situation. North Korean soldiers reportedly informed a work crew, tasked with cutting down the tree for visibility purposes, that such an action was forbidden. The reason given was deeply rooted in North Korean ideology and reverence for their leader: the tree, they claimed, had been personally planted by Kim Il Sung, the founding leader of North Korea. This assertion turned a simple tree into a symbol of national pride and propaganda, further complicating the already strained relations in the DMZ.

On the fateful day of August 18, 1976, a seemingly routine task in the Korean Demilitarized Zone escalated into a tragic and historic incident. In the Joint Security Area, a team composed of five Korean Service Corps personnel was tasked with pruning a poplar tree that had become a symbol of contention. They were escorted by a United Nations Command security team led by Captain Arthur Bonifas, along with his South Korean Army counterpart, Captain Kim. First Lieutenant Mark Barrett, the platoon leader of the current platoon in the area, and 11 enlisted personnel, a mix of American and South Korean soldiers, also joined the group.

Notably, the two captains did not carry sidearms, adhering to the protocol that limited the JSA to five armed officers and 30 armed enlisted personnel at any given time. However, in the back of their 2 1/2-ton truck were mattocks, and the KSC workers brought axes for the tree pruning task.

As the pruning commenced, the situation took a tense turn. Approximately 15 North Korean soldiers led by Senior Lieutenant Pak Chul, whom the UNC soldiers had nicknamed "Lieutenant Bulldog" due to his aggressive demeanor in past confrontations, appeared on the scene. Initially, Pak and his men seemed to observe the pruning without interference for about 15 minutes. Then, in a sudden shift, Pak ordered the UNC team to stop their work, claiming that the tree could not be pruned. Captain Bonifas, determined to complete the task, instructed his team to continue and dismissively turned his back on the North Koreans.

Feeling ignored, Pak sent a runner across the Bridge of No Return. Moments later, a truck carrying around 20 additional North Korean guards, equipped with crowbars and clubs, arrived at the scene. Pak repeated his demand to halt the pruning, but again, Bonifas turned his back, prompting a chilling response from Pak. After carefully wrapping and pocketing his watch, Pak gave a violent command: "Kill the bastards!"

What ensued was a brutal and swift attack. The North Korean forces, using axes left by the tree pruners, assaulted the UNC team. Both American soldiers, Bonifas and Barrett, were targeted, and almost all of the UNC guards sustained injuries. In a brutal act of violence, Bonifas was knocked down by Pak and then bludgeoned to death by at least five North Korean soldiers. Meanwhile, Barrett, in an attempt to escape, jumped over a low wall and disappeared into a 4.5-meter-deep depression filled with trees, obscured from view by dense grass and small trees.

The entire confrontation was shockingly brief, lasting only 20 to 30 seconds before the UNC forces were able to disperse the North Korean guards and retrieve Bonifas's body. Tragically, there was no immediate sign of Barrett, and he remained unseen by the two UNC guards stationed at Observation Post No. 5. This brutal incident, occurring within the politically charged environment of the DMZ, would leave a lasting impact on the relations between the North and South, underscoring the volatile nature of this heavily militarized border.

The aftermath of the brutal attack in the Korean Demilitarized Zone unfolded with a mix of urgency and confusion. The United Nations Command force, stationed at various observation posts, witnessed unsettling activities by the North Korean guards near the Korean People's Army No. 8 position along the UNC's emergency egress road. The behavior of these guards was peculiar and alarming: one guard would take an axe, disappear into the depression for a few minutes, then reemerge and hand the axe over to another guard, who would then repeat the process. This mysterious and ominous ritual continued for approximately 90 minutes.

During this time, a sudden and concerning realization dawned on the UNC guards at Observation Post No. 5: First Lieutenant Mark Barrett, who had been part of the tree-pruning detail, was unaccounted for. Upon learning of Barrett's absence, they quickly reported the suspicious activity they had been observing in the depression to their superiors. In response, a search-and-rescue squad was swiftly organized and dispatched to the area.

The rescue team's discovery was grim. They found that Barrett had been viciously attacked by the North Korean guards using an axe. In a critical condition, Barrett was rapidly evacuated, first to a nearby aid station at Camp Greaves and then transported to a hospital in Seoul. Tragically, despite these urgent efforts, Barrett succumbed to his injuries during the journey.

Meanwhile, Captain Shirron, who had stepped in to replace the fallen Captain Bonifas, along with Captain Shaddix, the joint duty officer's driver, the joint duty officer, and the guard at OP No. 5, witnessed the horrific attack from their observation post. In a desperate attempt to document the unfolding events, they used a black-and-white film camera to record the incident. Unfortunately, the film ran out midway through the recording. Captain Shaddix also used a 35 mm camera with a telephoto lens, providing a closer view of the chilling scene.

Simultaneously, the UNC guard stationed at Checkpoint No. 3, near the iconic Bridge of No Return, was also recording the incident, this time with a movie camera. These recordings would later serve as critical evidence of the brutal and unprovoked attack by the North Korean forces, highlighting the extreme tensions and the perilous nature of the DMZ.

In the immediate aftermath of the violent encounter in the Joint Security Area of the Korean Demilitarized Zone, a war of narratives ensued, with both sides presenting starkly different versions of the events. The North Korean media was quick to broadcast their account of the incident, framing it as an act of aggression by the United States. According to North Korean reports, at around 10:45 a.m., 14 "hoodlums with axes," presumably American soldiers, entered the Joint Security Area to cut down trees without prior mutual consent. When four North Korean personnel approached to dissuade them, the report claimed, they were violently attacked by the Americans, who were wielding "murderous weapons" and took advantage of their numerical superiority. The North Korean statement concluded by asserting that their guards were forced to engage in self-defense due to this "reckless provocation."

This narrative was further propagated on an international stage. Within just four hours of the incident, Kim Jong Il, the son of North Korean leader Kim Il Sung, addressed the Conference of Non-Aligned Nations in Colombo, Sri Lanka. He presented a prepared document that described the incident as an unprovoked attack on North Korean guards led by American officers. Exploiting this platform, Kim Jong Il introduced a resolution seeking to condemn the United States for the day's events. He called for the withdrawal of US forces from Korea and the dissolution of the United Nations Command. This resolution, backed by Cuba, found support among the members of the conference, who passed it, signaling a significant diplomatic setback for the United States.

On the other side, the United States and its allies viewed the incident through a drastically different lens. The Central Intelligence Agency assessed that the attack was premeditated and orchestrated by the North Korean government. In response to this grave incident, a range of potential retaliatory measures was considered. The readiness levels for American forces in South Korea were escalated to DEFCON 3 early on August 19, indicating a heightened state of military preparedness. Although more aggressive options like rocket and artillery attacks were contemplated, these were ultimately dismissed due to the unfavorable artillery ratio of 4:1 against the UNC forces. Moreover, South Korean President Park Chung Hee, wary of escalating military tensions, expressed his preference against taking military action.

Operation Paul Bunyan, a decisive and dramatic response to the tragic killings in the Korean Demilitarized Zone, unfolded on August 21 at 07:00, just three days after the harrowing incident. Named after the legendary American folk hero, the operation was a bold show of force and determination. Task Force Vierra, named in honor of Lieutenant Colonel Victor S. Vierra, commander of the United States Army Support Group, led the operation. In a move that took the North Koreans by surprise, a convoy of 23 American and South Korean vehicles rolled into the Joint Security Area without prior warning. The timing was strategically chosen, as the North Koreans had only one observation post staffed at that early hour.

The heart of the operation was two eight-man teams of military engineers from the 2nd Engineer Battalion, 2nd Infantry Division. These engineers, equipped with chain saws, had a clear mission: to cut down the contentious tree that had been at the center of the fatal confrontation. Alongside them, two 30-man security platoons from the Joint Security Force were prepared for any eventuality. These platoons, armed with pistols and axe handles, had specific roles: the 1st Platoon was tasked with securing the northern entrance to the JSA via the Bridge of No Return, while the 2nd Platoon took charge of the southern edge.

Simultaneously, a meticulously planned military operation was underway. Captain Walter Seifried of B Company had activated the detonation systems for the explosives on Freedom Bridge. The main gun of the M728 combat engineer vehicle was aimed squarely at the middle of the bridge, ready to bring it down if necessary. In parallel, B Company, supporting E Company (bridge), was constructing M4T6 rafts on the Imjin River, preparing for a potential emergency evacuation.

But the operation had another, more startling element. A 64-man task force from the Republic of Korea Army's 1st Special Forces Brigade, known for their expertise in taekwondo and ostensibly unarmed, accompanied the convoy. However, upon arriving near the Bridge of No Return, a surprising and intimidating tactic was revealed. The soldiers swiftly removed sandbags from the bottoms of their trucks, uncovering concealed M16 rifles and M79 grenade launchers. This unexpected armament significantly upped the ante of the operation. Some commandos took their show of force even further by strapping M18 Claymore mines to their chests, holding the firing mechanism in their hands, and boldly challenging the North Koreans to cross the bridge.

The scale and intensity of the military response following the tragic incident in the Korean Demilitarized Zone were unprecedented, showcasing a formidable display of military might. The operation, named after Lieutenant Colonel Victor S. Vierra, commander of the United States Army Support Group, was a resounding declaration of strength and preparedness by the US and South Korean forces.

Above the Joint Security Area, the skies were filled with an impressive array of military aircraft. A US infantry company was transported by 20 utility helicopters, flanked by seven Cobra attack helicopters, each maneuvering with precision and purpose. This aerial armada was just the beginning. Behind these helicopters, B-52 Stratofortresses, long-range bombers hailing all the way from Guam, majestically cruised through the sky. They were escorted by a squadron of US F-4 Phantom IIs from Kunsan Air Base, a testament to the seriousness of the response. Adding to this aerial fortress, South Korean F-5 and F-86 fighters cut across the sky at high altitudes, a visible and potent symbol of the combined military capabilities of the allies.

The show of force was further bolstered by additional air support from various bases. F-4Es from Osan Air Base and Taegu Air Base in South Korea were strategically positioned, alongside F-111 bombers from the 366th Tactical Fighter Wing out of Mountain Home Air Force Base. Further support came from F-4C and F-4D Phantoms from the 18th Tactical Fighter Wing at Kadena Air Base and Clark Air Base. The USS Midway, an aircraft carrier, and its task force were also moved into a strategic offshore position, ready to provide necessary support.

On the ground, the display of military preparedness was equally impressive. Near the edges of the Demilitarized Zone, heavily armed US and South Korean infantry units, artillery, including the Second Battalion, 71st Air Defense Regiment armed with Improved Hawk missiles, and armored units were in position, ready to support the special operations team. Military bases near the DMZ were on high alert, with preparations for demolition in case of a hostile military response. The DEFCON was elevated on the orders of General Stilwell, as would be later detailed in Colonel De LaTeur's research paper. Furthermore, 12,000 additional troops were ordered to Korea, including 1,800 Marines from Okinawa. During the operation, the ominous presence of nuclear-capable strategic bombers circling over the JSA added a grave and serious tone to the proceedings.

Task Force Vierra, the heart of this operation, was a formidable force consisting of 813 men. This included almost all members of the United States Army Support Group, to which the Joint Security Force belonged, a South Korean reconnaissance company, a South Korean Special Forces company that had stealthily infiltrated the river area by the bridge the night before, and members of a reinforced composite rifle company from the 9th Infantry Regiment. In tandem with this, every United Nations Command force throughout South Korea was on battle alert, signifying a unified and ready stance in the face of potential conflict.

The execution of Operation Paul Bunyan was a masterclass in military precision and psychological strategy, transforming a simple task of cutting down a tree into an assertive demonstration of force. The engineers involved in this critical operation were from two adept teams belonging to B Company and C Company of the 2nd Engineer Battalion. They were expertly led by First Lieutenant Patrick Ono, who had previously reconnoitered the tree while undercover, cleverly disguised as a Korean corporal just two days earlier. Their mission was straightforward yet highly symbolic – to cut down the contentious tree that had sparked the deadly incident.

Upon arrival at the Joint Security Area, the engineers wasted no time. They disembarked from their vehicles and immediately set to work. In a display of resourcefulness, they stood atop their truck to reach the towering tree. Meanwhile, the 2nd Platoon truck strategically positioned itself to block the Bridge of No Return, a critical choke point in the area. The rest of the task force dispersed efficiently to their designated positions around the tree, each unit assuming its role in safeguarding the engineers as they worked.

North Korea's response was swift but measured. Approximately 150 to 200 North Korean troops, equipped with machine guns and assault rifles, arrived at the scene. Initially, they remained within their buses, observing the unfolding events with cautious attention. It was at this juncture that Lieutenant Colonel Vierra, sensing the escalating tension, relayed a crucial radio communication. In response, helicopters and Air Force jets emerged over the horizon, a visible and powerful show of support. Meanwhile, Yokota Air Base in Japan was on full alert, with the runway lined with a dozen C-130s, ready to provide immediate backup if needed.

The North Korean troops eventually disembarked from their buses and began setting up machine gun positions in pairs. From these vantage points, they silently watched as the tree was methodically felled. The operation, completed in a mere 42 minutes – three minutes less than General Stilwell's estimate – successfully avoided any violent confrontation. During this time, two road barriers installed by the North Koreans were removed, and South Korean troops carried out acts of vandalism on two North Korean guard posts. Symbolically, a 6-meter-tall stump of the tree was left standing, a stark reminder of the day's events.

Five minutes into the operation, the United Nations Command notified North Korea in the JSA about a UN work party finishing the August 18 task. This message and the display of force had a psychological impact. The operation, beyond just trimming a tree, was a strategic deterrent, signaling resolve and readiness to counter aggression, impacting beyond the DMZ.

Clementine Barnabet

In the waning days of January 1911, a chilling incident unfolded in the quiet town of West Crowley, Louisiana, sending shockwaves through the community. The scene was set at a modest residence located at 605 Western Avenue, where a sense of foreboding loomed in the air. On that fateful afternoon, a police officer, identified as Officer Ballew, was summoned through an urgent, anxiety-laden phone call. The neighbors, gripped by a mix of fear and suspicion, had raised alarms about a potential tragedy at the address.

Upon his arrival, Officer Ballew was confronted with a horrifying tableau. Inside, he discovered the lifeless bodies of the home's three inhabitants— a man, a woman, and a young boy. The family lay in their bed, each with their skulls brutally fractured. The scene was macabre: the bed saturated with blood, the floor scattered with ghastly footprints, all pointing towards a heinous crime committed under the veil of night. The investigation revealed that all entry points were secured, suggesting a nightmarish reality where the perpetrator had stealthily entered through a window and executed the family in their sleep.

Further adding to the grim atmosphere was a bucket filled with blood, ominously placed in one corner of the room. Near the head of the bed, towering over the victims, stood a blood-stained ax, the silent witness to the atrocity.

This gruesome event was not an isolated incident but part of a series of ax murders that had begun to cast a shadow of terror over parts of Louisiana and Texas during the early 1910s. These crimes were steeped in mystery and dark folklore, with whispers of a deranged Voodoo priestess and a sinister cult known as the "Church of Sacrifice." It was rumored that this group engaged in macabre rituals, sacrificing their victims in bizarre ceremonies.

The local newspaper, capturing the horror and disbelief of the community, declared the incident at 605 Western Avenue "the most brutal murder in the history of this section." As the investigation deepened, suspicion initially fell upon several men. However, the case took an unexpected turn when the perpetrator was revealed to be an African-American woman named Clementine Barnabet. Her connection to Voodoo, if any, was tenuous, but her confession was shocking. Barnabet admitted to the cold-blooded murder of 35 people, though the exact number of her victims remains shrouded in mystery.

As the second decade of the 20th century dawned, a series of harrowing murders began to unfold, casting a shadow of fear and uncertainty over a string of towns dotting the Southern Pacific railroad line. These gruesome events, which would later be linked in a web of terror and mystery, commenced with what some sources suggest was the inaugural crime of this horrifying saga— the murder of Edna Opelousas and her three children in Rayne, Louisiana, in November 1909.

This initial act of violence, however, was merely the prelude to a series of killings that would escalate in brutality and frequency. The next incident occurred in late January 1911, when the small town of Crowley, Louisiana, became the backdrop for a chilling crime. Walter Byers, his wife, and their son were brutally murdered, hacked to death in a manner that was shocking even to the police, who were no strangers to crime in their impoverished part of town. The phrase "brained with an ax" disturbingly encapsulated the viciousness of the attack.

The nightmare continued on February 25, when the murderer struck again. This time, the Andrus family of Lafayette, Louisiana, fell victim, with four of its members being mercilessly killed. The police, piecing together the similarities in these crimes, began to suspect that they were dealing with a serial killer, a "terrible monster" whose bloodlust knew no bounds.

March brought another ghastly chapter to this saga, this time in San Antonio, Texas. The Casaway family—Alfred, Elizabeth, and their three children— were all murdered in a manner strikingly similar to the previous killings.

The investigation into these crimes initially led to a few false leads, but eventually, the focus shifted to Raymond Barnabet, a petty criminal and sharecropper from Lafayette. Residing in a less affluent part of town, Raymond became a prime suspect following accusations from his mistress, who, after a quarrel, hinted at his potential involvement in the murders.

During Raymond's trial in October 1911, the case took a dramatic turn when his children, Zepherin and Clementine Barnabet, testified against their father. The teenage Clementine gave a chilling testimony, recounting an evening when her father returned home covered in blood, issuing threats to the family. Zepherin corroborated her story, adding the haunting detail that their father boasted about killing the Andrus family. Both siblings expressed a palpable fear for their lives if their father were to be released.

However, while Raymond was incarcerated, another murder occurred, further complicating the case. On November 26, 1911, the Randall family in Lafayette suffered a fate similar to the previous victims. Norbert Randall, his wife, their three children, and a nephew were all savagely murdered. This time, there was a chilling deviation: while the family was attacked with an ax, Norbert Randall was additionally shot in the head.

The unsettling string of murders had unequivocally established that a ruthless killer was still at large, casting a shadow of dread over the community. In the midst of this alarming situation, Lafayette Parish Sheriff Louis LaCoste found himself grappling with a growing suspicion towards Raymond Barnabet's children. Their arrest was not just a twist in the investigation but a reflection of the unease that had permeated the town.

Sheriff LaCoste's suspicions were not unfounded. In the community, the Barnabet siblings had garnered a notorious reputation. During Raymond's trial, their own neighbors, the Stevens family, painted a grim portrait of them, describing them as "filthy, shifty, degenerate"—words that reverberated with condemnation and suspicion. But it wasn't just their reputation that raised eyebrows; there was tangible evidence that implicated them, particularly Clementine.

A significant piece of this puzzle emerged during Raymond's arrest at the Barnabet residence. The police made a chilling discovery: bloodstains from the Andrus murders on Clementine's clothes. Clementine had offered an explanation during her father's trial, claiming Raymond had wiped the blood on her clothing. However, Sheriff LaCoste harbored doubts about this version of events, sensing that the truth might be more sinister.

These doubts gained further credibility when deputies conducted a thorough search of the Barnabet family home after arresting Clementine. According to a November 28, 1911 report in The Daily Picayune, the search yielded a horrifying find—a complete suit of woman's clothes in Clementine's room, not just stained, but saturated with blood and spattered with human brains. This gruesome discovery was compounded by another macabre detail: the latch on their door was also covered in blood.

While Zepherin managed to provide an alibi for the night of the murders, Clementine's lack of an alibi placed her under a cloud of grave suspicion. With no defense for her whereabouts, she was taken into custody and incarcerated.

However, in a turn of events that only deepened the horror and mystery of the situation, the murders continued even after Clementine's arrest. The persistence of these killings, despite the arrest of a prime suspect, suggested a complexity to the case that baffled and unnerved the authorities and the public alike.

In the grim winter of January 1912, a new wave of terror swept through Louisiana as three more families fell victim to the relentless brutality of an unknown murderer or murderers. Among these tragic incidents, the murder of the Broussard family in Lake Charles stood out for its particularly macabre details. Felix Broussard, his wife, and their three children were not only slain but found with their hands eerily splayed apart, held in place by pieces of wood. This chilling scene was further compounded by a cryptic message left on the wall.

The message's contents added a layer of ominous mystery to the already horrifying scene. Depending on the source, it was either written in blood or pencil, but its words were equally haunting regardless of the medium. The message was a paraphrase of Psalm 9:12 from the King James Bible: "When he maketh the inquisition for blood, he forgetteth not the cry of the humble." The signature accompanying this message, "Human Five," sparked a chilling hypothesis among the police and the public: that these heinous acts were the work of a group, now infamously dubbed by the press as The Human Five Gang.

The media frenzy that ensued was both sensational and speculative. Newspapers across the country latched onto the story, with the El Paso Gazette being one of the first to propose a connection between the murders and Voodoo rituals. Their coverage, under the headline "Voodoo's Horrors Break Out Again," suggested a link to human sacrifices performed as part of Voodoo ceremonies. The story emphasized the number five as having significant ritualistic importance, weaving a narrative of calculated, ritualistic killings. The Gazette erroneously reported that each of these sacrifices targeted five family members, citing the Wexford family tragedy as an example, where they claimed an infant was not considered in the ritual due to its age. This reporting, however, was not entirely accurate as the number of victims in these families typically ranged from four to six.

The Voodoo theory propagated by the El Paso Gazette found traction in other local newspapers, fueling widespread speculation and fear. Concurrently, rumors began to circulate about Clementine Barnabet being the leader of a mysterious cult referred to as the "Church of Sacrifice." This shadowy group was purportedly linked to Reverend King Harris, a Pentecostal preacher associated with the Christ Sanctified Holy Church. When the police interrogated Reverend Harris amidst the frenzy of religious speculation, he was reportedly shocked and dismayed. He vehemently denied any knowledge of a so-called "Church of Sacrifice" and was visibly distressed at the thought that his sermons could have been misconstrued as inspiration for such gruesome acts.

The perplexing and grisly case of the ax murders that had haunted Southern Louisiana began to unravel with a significant breakthrough in April 1912. On the 5th of that month, Clementine Barnabet, a central figure in this disturbing saga, made a startling confession, admitting her involvement in 17 murders. This admission opened a window into a world of dark rituals and clandestine activities that had thus far eluded investigators.

Clementine's confession, as reported in The Daily Picayune, was as chilling as it was revealing. She claimed to have purchased a Voodoo charm, believing it would offer her protection while committing these heinous crimes. She described a grim process where she and her alleged accomplices would draw lots to determine who would carry out the murders. One of the more disturbing aspects of her confession was her admission of disguising herself as a man, a tactic employed to move undetected in the night.

Perhaps the most harrowing detail in her confession was her rationale for murdering the children. She expressed a twisted sense of mercy, claiming she killed them to spare them the fate of being orphans in the world. However, the deeper motives behind these brutal acts remained shrouded in mystery.

The Lafayette Advertiser, in its April 5, 1912 edition, published Clementine's full confession. However, the paper expressed skepticism, highlighting the inconsistencies in her story and her previous misleading statements regarding her accomplices. This skepticism was fueled by her earlier testimony against her father and the continued occurrence of murders even after his incarceration.

Sheriff LaCoste's investigation into the accomplices named by Clementine led to several dead ends. Arrests were made, but the search for the other members of the so-called "Human Five Gang" proved fruitless, casting doubt on the existence of such a group.

District Attorney Howard E. Bruner, analyzing the pattern of the murders, suggested that some might have been committed by copycats. Nevertheless, he was convinced of Clementine's guilt, particularly disturbed by her admission of post-mortem desecration of the victims.

The complex web of facts, rumors, and myths surrounding the case was further explored in a summary published by The Federal Writers Project in 1942. This account clarified the widespread public confusion and misinformation that had permeated the case. Notably, it dispelled the existence of the so-called "Church of Sacrifice." The confusion seemed to stem from a mix-up between Reverend Harris's Sanctified Church and the fictitious Sacrifice Church, exacerbated by the rampant rumors of Voodoo cults. Reverend Harris, who had preached in Lafayette on the night of the Randall murders, was found to be uninvolved in the crimes.

The tragic and sensationalized events surrounding the ax murders in Louisiana had irreversibly woven a narrative that intertwined crime with elements of Voodoo mysticism, leaving an indelible mark on the community of Lafayette. The townsfolk, already reeling from the shock and horror of the murders, found it all too easy to accept the theory of a Voodoo priestess orchestrating these heinous crimes as part of a sacrificial cult. This narrative was further fueled by Clementine Barnabet's confession, in which she implicated a certain Joseph Thibodeaux as the provider of an invisibility charm and the instigator of the crimes.

Thibodeaux, however, vehemently denied these allegations. Far from being a Voodoo priest, he claimed his practices were limited to root-based medicine, a detail corroborated by local reports which described him as a peaceful individual known more for benign practices like conjuring warts away rather than any involvement in dark rituals.

Despite the dubious nature of Clementine's confession and the inconsistencies in her story, the tales about her continued to spread. On April 14, 1912, District Attorney Howard E. Bruner officially filed charges against her. As she awaited trial in jail, Clementine's narrative evolved, with her confessing to as many as 35 murders. Yet, each retelling of her story introduced new discrepancies, casting further doubt on the veracity of her claims.

The question of Clementine's mental state became a focal point of her defense. Her attorneys argued for her insanity, but despite this plea, she was tried, found guilty, and sentenced to life imprisonment at the Louisiana Penitentiary at the young age of 19. Her time in prison was marked by a brief escape attempt on July 31, 1913, which ended with her recapture on the same day. Interestingly, despite this incident, she was regarded as a model prisoner during her incarceration.

Clementine's prison tenure, however, was surprisingly short-lived. Reports emerged of a mysterious "procedure" she underwent while in prison, which was alleged to have "restored" her to a "normal condition." This supposed rehabilitation, coupled with her good behavior, led to her release after serving just a decade behind bars.

The story of Clementine Barnabet, steeped in layers of mystery, folklore, and sensational journalism, left a complex legacy. It not only reflected the societal fears and stereotypes of the time but also highlighted the challenges in discerning truth from myth in the realm of crime and punishment. The blend of fact and fiction in her story continued to stir debate and curiosity, symbolizing a dark chapter in the history of Louisiana and the American South.

Billy the Axeman

The notion of a roaming murderer, dubbed "Billy the Axeman" by the press in 1911, captivated the American Midwest with its sinister implications. Journalists and investigators began linking a series of gruesome axe murders based on chilling commonalities: whole families were being slaughtered, the proximity of the crimes to railways, and the consistent use of an axe as the murder weapon. This pattern led many to speculate about the existence of a single, itinerant killer.

Special Agent Matthew Wilson McClaughry of the Department of Justice seized upon this theory in an attempt to associate Henry Lee Moore's 1912 axe murders with this broader pattern. However, his efforts ultimately failed to produce conclusive results, and no individual was ever convicted for more than one of these heinous crimes. Despite this, the myth of this serial killer continued to intrigue true crime enthusiasts, bloggers, and podcasters for decades.

In 2015, author Todd Elliott brought a new dimension to this mystery. He expanded the investigation to include similar axe murders that occurred in Texas and Louisiana between 1911 and 1912. Elliott noted startling similarities in these cases: entire families were annihilated in the dead of night, typically with the blunt side of an axe, and the crime scenes were often near railways. However, a distinct and disturbing pattern emerged in the southern states – the victims were predominantly black and mixed-race families. Elliott posited that these murders were likely the work of the same perpetrator.

The theory took another turn in 2017 with the publication of "The Man from the Train" by authors Bill James and Rachel McCarthy James. They argued that the series of murders likely extended even further back in time than previously thought. The authors suggested that the earliest crimes displayed a level of sophistication indicative of an experienced killer. Their book not only expanded the timeline of these murders but also introduced a new suspect, adding another layer to this complex and haunting historical mystery.

In the early 1900s, axes were commonplace in households and, alarmingly, became a frequent weapon of choice in numerous murders. To differentiate the Midwest murder series from other unrelated axe homicides, various authors have meticulously outlined specific characteristics and patterns that suggest these crimes were the work of a singular individual. Beth Klingensmith was among the first to methodically compile these traits.

Klingensmith's research reveals a hauntingly consistent pattern: the murders occurred predominantly on Sunday nights in small towns. The murderer, believed to be a train hopper, would strategically select a target house based on certain criteria. After careful observation and ensuring the residents were asleep, he would then enter the home, usually through an unlocked door or a rear window, often removing the screen and leaning it against the wall.

The killer used an axe found at the scene or nearby as his murder weapon - a chilling example of opportunistic brutality. Once inside, he used the household's own lamp for illumination, meticulously adjusting it by removing the chimney and lowering the wick to avoid detection. The assailant covered the faces of his victims, possibly to minimize blood splatter, and executed them with swift, blunt blows to the head using the axe.

After the murders, the killer engaged in a macabre ritual: washing his hands, obscuring the windows, rearranging and further mutilating the bodies, and often covering them post-mortem. His attacks were specifically targeted at the heads and faces, leaving the rest of the bodies untouched. Before making his escape, he meticulously cleaned the axe of fingerprints, left it at the crime scene, and secured the house to impede discovery. The killer then vanished as quickly as he arrived, usually by catching a train on the nearby railway line, continuing his grim journey.

Bill James and Rachel McCarthy James expanded upon the research framework set by Beth Klingensmith, introducing revisions and hypothesizing deeper motivations behind the crimes. They noted a disturbing pattern where a young female victim, often a prepubescent girl, was found in a sexually explicit position at the end of the bed. This observation, coupled with the period's newspaper accounts that hinted at post-mortem assaults, suggested elements of necrophilia and pedophilia in the crimes.

The authors also proposed the killer's possible aversion to human faces. This theory was supported by his actions of mutilating victims' faces, covering their faces post-mortem, obscuring mirrors, and even covering telephones, which in that era often bore a resemblance to human faces.

They observed a distinct evolution in the crime series. In the later series (1909-1912), the murders took place in small towns, and the houses were often locked up post-crime. Contrastingly, the earlier series (1900-1906) predominantly featured remote farmstead murders, where the killer typically set the house ablaze.

James and McCarthy James suggested different methodologies for selecting victims in each series. In the early series, the killer possibly settled in a location temporarily, worked in logging or mining, and scouted potential targets. After his work contract ended, he committed the murders. In the later Midwest series, he appeared to randomly select a house in a small town after briefly observing it from a train.

They also noted the proximity of many crime scenes to logging and mining operations, suggesting the killer's familiarity with axes or pickaxes. Furthermore, the lack of financial motive was evident as victims were often impoverished, or if not, valuables were left untouched at the crime scene.

Other authors have speculated on the killer's physical characteristics. Some posited that he couldn't have been tall, as he maneuvered an axe in confined indoor spaces, supported by size six footprints found at one crime scene. Analysis of the attack patterns led to the hypothesis that the killer might have been left-handed. Aaron Mahnke, from the Lore podcast, even speculated that the killer might have wiped his fingerprints because they were already on record due to a previous incarceration.

In the summer of 1911, two family murders in the Northwest, one in Ardenwald, Oregon, and the other in Rainier, Washington, occurred just months before the main series of Midwestern murders. Initially, the press linked these crimes to the Midwestern series, but W. M. McClaughry later dismissed them from his theory. Modern authors remain divided, with some suggesting a connection and others expressing skepticism.

The Hill family in Ardenwald, Oregon, met a tragic end on the night of June 9 to 10, 1911. The victims were William Hill, 34, his wife Ruth Hill, 33, and Ruth's children from a previous marriage, Philip Rintoul, 9, and Dorothy Rintoul, 4. They were brutally murdered in their beds, with fatal blows to their heads delivered by an axe found at the scene. The crime was believed to have occurred shortly after midnight, inferred from a neighbor's dog barking around that time. Post-mortem, the bodies were moved and covered; both Dorothy and Ruth were sexually assaulted, with bloody fingerprints found on Dorothy's body and Ruth's body positioned at the end of the bed. The perpetrator washed up at the scene and covered the windows.

The crime was discovered the next morning by a neighbor, leading to a series of suspects being investigated. One suspect, neighbor Nathan Harvey, was charged in 1912 but was ultimately acquitted.

On the night of July 9 to 10, 1911, the Coble family in Rainier, Washington, suffered a similar fate. The victims, Archie Coble, 28, and his wife Nettie Coble, 18, were murdered in their beds, also with an axe. The killer covered Archie's face post-murder, and Nettie was assaulted after death. Blood found on the chimney of the oil lamp at the scene indicated the killer had interacted with it. Due to the similarities, the press linked these murders with the Hill family's.

Several suspects were investigated, including a Swedish immigrant working on the nearby railroad and his foreman, George Wilson. Both implicated themselves during interrogation, and eventually, Wilson was convicted of the crime. However, doubts about his guilt persist to this day.

The central sequence of the Midwestern murder series spanned from September 1911 to June 1912, beginning in Colorado Springs, Colorado, and extending across various small towns, all strategically situated along major railway lines. This series was marked by the brutal murders of several families, starting with the Burnham and Wayne families in Colorado Springs and progressing through the Dawson family in Monmouth, Illinois, the Showman family in Ellsworth, Kansas, the Hudson family in Paola, Kansas, and culminating in the horrific murder of the Moore family and two visiting girls in Villisca, Iowa.

Colorado Springs, the initial site of this series, was the largest town involved, with a population just shy of 30,000 in 1911. The other towns were smaller but shared a key feature: their robust connections to the railway network, which was a critical aspect of the killer's modus operandi.

The series commenced on the night of September 17-18, 1911, with two simultaneous family murders in Colorado Springs. The victims were the Burnham family—May Alice Burnham, 35, and her children, Nellie, 7, and John, 2—and the Wayne family—Henry F. Wayne, 24, his wife Blanche, 22, and their eighteen-month-old daughter Lula. Both families were visiting the city, staying in cottages while the men were at the local Modern Woodmen of

America Sanatorium.

The gruesome discovery of the murders was made on the morning of September 20. In both cases, the victims had been bludgeoned with the blunt side of an axe, and their faces were covered with bed sheets. The murder weapon was sourced from one of the houses and left at the scene. The murderer had meticulously covered the windows and jammed the houses shut before departing. Signs indicated that the killer had remained at the crime scenes for some time, cleaning up and removing any fingerprints from the murder weapon. Proximity to the railway line, just a few houses away, was a notable aspect of these crime scenes.

Robbery was quickly dismissed as a motive, as nothing of value was taken from either house. Additionally, no personal motives could be established, as both families were temporary residents with no known enemies in the area. Initial suspicion fell on Mr. Burnham, the sole surviving member of the Burnham family, but he was quickly cleared due to his confirmed presence at the sanatorium, battling tuberculosis.

The subsequent tragedy in this series unfolded on the night of September 30 to October 1, 1911, in Monmouth, Illinois. The Dawson family, comprising William Dawson, 56, his wife Charity, 52, and their 12-year-old daughter Georgia, became the next victims. The Dawsons resided in the area south of the railroad tracks, known locally as the "colored" part of town, though the Dawsons were white. William Dawson worked as a janitor at the local First United Presbyterian Church.

The crime came to light when Dawson failed to show up for his Sunday morning duties at the church, prompting concerned congregation members to investigate. They discovered the family in their beds, each brutally beaten to death. Reports indicated that the killer had covered the windows and the victims post-mortem, and had also disturbingly positioned Georgia Dawson at the end of her bed.

Initially, an axe was suspected as the murder weapon, but a subsequent investigation led authorities to believe a gas pipe was used instead. This conclusion came after bloodhounds traced the killer's scent to a pond near the railroad, where the pipe was discovered. Intriguingly, a pocket flashlight was later found near a fence along the path indicated by the bloodhounds. It bore an inscription with the words "Loving", "Lovey", or a similar variation, alongside "Colorado Springs" and the date "Sept. 4, '11", which the press linked to the earlier Colorado Springs murders.

Authorities explored revenge as a possible motive. Two men, John Wesley Knight and Lovey Mitchell, were subsequently charged based on the flashlight inscription and witness testimony. While Lovey Mitchell was eventually acquitted after multiple trials, John Wesley Knight was convicted and sentenced to 19 years in prison.

On the night of October 15 to 16, 1911, the Showman family in Ellsworth, Kansas, fell victim to a heinous crime. William Showman, 31, his wife Pauline, 26, and their three children, Lester, 6, Fern, 4, and Fenton, 1, were all found murdered. William was employed as a chauffeur in the town.

The bodies were discovered on the afternoon of October 16. Each family member had been killed with the blunt side of an axe, their heads brutally crushed. Their small cabin, located very close to a railway line, became the scene of this grim act. The killer had taken the time to cover all windows and the telephone, leaving no visible signs of theft from the house. Pauline Showman's body was found positioned in a sexually explicit manner post-mortem. At the crime scene, police found the murder weapon, which had been wiped clean of fingerprints, and a lamp with its chimney removed, discovered under a chair in the kitchen.

Following the trail of the murders, bloodhounds led investigators to a nearby intersection of two railway lines. Additionally, an attempted break-in was reported at the home of city marshal Morris Merritt. In the morning, he found a removed screen and an attempted forced entry at his window. His house was just adjacent to the railroad and merely two houses away from the Showmans'.

This incident was the first where the press began to draw connections between various crimes, coining the term "Billy the Axman" for the suspected perpetrator. However, local police focused on nearby suspects. Charles Marzyck, Pauline Showman's former brother-in-law who had previously threatened the family, was apprehended but released after his alibi was verified. Another suspect was a man known as John Smith or John Smitherton, who had stayed at a local hotel the night of the murders and left behind a bundle of clothes. He was located and interviewed by the police, during which he claimed to have found the clothes near the railway lines upon disembarking from a train on the evening of the murders. Authors Bill James and Rachel McCarthy James have speculated that these clothes could have belonged to the actual murderer, used as a disguise to escape.

On the night of June 5 to 6, 1912, a tragic event unfolded in Paola, Kansas, claiming the lives of Rollin Hudson, 21, and his wife Anna, 22. The young couple, who had moved to Paola in the spring of 1912, reportedly faced marital issues, partly attributed to suspicions of Anna's infidelity. Initially living with another family, they soon moved into their own house.

The discovery of the murders occurred the following day when, concerned by Mr. Hudson's absence from work, a group of women forced entry into the Hudson home. They found Rollin and Anna Hudson dead, their skulls brutally crushed. The killer had gained entry through a rear window, carefully removing and leaning the screen against the house. Inside, he lit a coal lamp, removed its chimney, and placed it beneath the bed. The bodies were covered post-mortem, and the murder weapon, believed to be a blunt instrument like a pickaxe or hammer, was never found. The absence of stolen items ruled out robbery as a motive.

That same night, a foiled attack occurred at the nearby Longmeyer family home. Here too, the intruder entered through a rear window, removing the screen and lighting an oil lamp. However, this attack was interrupted when Mrs. Longmeyer awoke to the sound of breaking glass, causing the intruder to flee. The source of the noise was the lamp's chimney. Both the Hudson and Longmeyer residences were a short walk from the junction of two railway lines.

Despite the parallels to the previous murders, public suspicion initially gravitated towards local men, speculated to be involved with Anna Hudson. However, the Sheriff noted the similarities in the modus operandi and the sophistication of the attacks, linking them to the earlier series of murders. Despite these connections, no one was ever charged for the Hudson murders.

The final horrific event in the Midwestern murder series occurred on the night of June 9 to 10, 1912, in Villisca, Iowa. The victims were the Moore family—Josiah, 43, his wife Sara, 39, and their four children Herman, 11, Katherine, 10, Boyd, 7, and Paul, 5. Additionally, two young guests, Lena Stillinger, 11, and Ina Stillinger, 8, friends of the Moore children, were also slain during a sleepover.

The gruesome scene was uncovered the next morning when a neighbor, noticing an unusual stillness at the Moore house, alerted Josiah Moore's brother. Upon entering the house, he discovered that all the occupants had been bludgeoned to death with the blunt side of an axe. It's believed the killer entered through an unlocked back door. Inside, he lit a lamp, removed the chimney, and placed it under a chair. The murders were carried out with swift brutality, leaving all victims in their beds. The killer covered the faces of the victims, mirrors, windows, and a telephone, before washing his hands. Lena Stillinger's body was positioned in a sexually explicit manner, and there was evidence suggesting the killer may have committed an indecent act over her body. The axe, taken from within the house, was left at the scene. No items of value were stolen.

Similar to previous incidents in Colorado Springs, Ellsworth, and Paola, there was a possible second attempt that same night. At 2:10 AM, Villisca resident Xenia Delaney was awakened by the sound of someone attempting to enter her room, but finding the door locked, the intruder retreated.

The discovery of the Moore family and the Stillinger girls led to a police investigation with bloodhounds, which traced a trail to a railway junction. Initially linked to the other crimes in the series, the focus quickly shifted to local suspects. George J. Kelly, an English immigrant, was one of those tried but eventually acquitted.

Subsequent crimes have led some authors to ponder if they could be extensions of this series. For instance, the Pfannschmidt murders on September 27, 1912, involved the killing of the Pfannschmidt family in their beds, followed by the burning of their house. The sole survivor, Ray Pfannschmidt, implicated "Billy the Axeman" in his defense. Another case is the Kellar family murders on June 10, 1913, where the family was similarly killed in their beds.

Henry Lee Moore, who was convicted in 1913 for the axe murders of his mother and grandmother in Missouri, drew the attention of Special Agent W. M. McClaughry due to similarities in his crime and the fact that he was released just before the Colorado Springs murders. However, recent authors have cast doubt on his involvement in the wider Midwest axe murders.

Charles Marzyck, a former brother-in-law of Pauline Showman, was a suspect in her family's murder. Allegations of his connections to Monmouth and Colorado Springs led to speculation about his involvement in those murders as well. Police apprehended Marzyck and brought him to Ellsworth, but he provided evidence of his innocence and was released.

Lovey Mitchell faced two trials for the 1911 Monmouth murders and was linked by the press to other murders in the series. Ultimately, he was declared innocent and released in 1918. However, Philip Jenkins later suggested

Mitchell was responsible for the Midwest axe murders in a review article on historical serial killers.

George Kelly, an English-born traveling minister, was a prime suspect in the Villisca Axe Murders, the last and most notorious of the Midwestern series. Although he was tried and acquitted, Todd Elliott speculated that Kelly could be the serial killer behind both the Midwestern and Southern series of murders, noting religious elements in the Southern crimes.

Paul Müller, a German-born farmhand, emerged as a suspect in the 1898 Newton family slaying and was the subject of an extensive manhunt. Authors Bill James and Rachel McCarthy James, in their 2017 book, identified him as the most likely perpetrator of the axe murders, a conclusion supported by Harold Schechter, who called it the "most probable solution".

Bill James and Rachel McCarthy James also noted that the later crimes in the series exhibited a mature modus operandi, indicative of an experienced serial killer. They hypothesized that the first crime in the series would likely reveal some novice mistakes while still encompassing the main characteristics of the later crimes. They argue that the Newton family murders fit this description, thereby aligning with their theory of Müller's involvement.

Stephen Richards the Nebraska Fiend

The mid-19th century was a pivotal era for Nebraska, marked by significant changes and developments. The passage of the Kansas-Nebraska Act in 1854 was a critical moment in the region's history. This act led to the establishment of Nebraska and Kansas territories, primarily to support the construction of the Transcontinental Railroad. This infrastructure project was not just a feat of engineering; it symbolized the nation's expansion and ambition.

In 1867, two years after the end of the American Civil War, Nebraska's journey as a territory culminated in its admission to the Union as the 37th state. This milestone was more than a political formality; it represented a new chapter in the region's history. The statehood of Nebraska attracted a wave of settlers, drawn by the promise of opportunity and growth. This influx of people significantly altered the demographic and political landscape of the area.

Amidst this backdrop of change, Nebraska's first governor, David Butler, played a controversial yet instrumental role. His governance was a catalyst for political debates and reforms, including the push for a new state constitution in 1871. These reforms were not merely administrative; they reflected the evolving identity and aspirations of Nebraska's people.

This period also saw the gradual development of Nebraska's legal and judicial system. In the early years of statehood, the legal framework was still in its infancy. The state's criminal code, a cornerstone of its legal system, was only formally established in 1871. This nascent legal system was tested by the crimes and subsequent trial of an individual named Richards. His case was noteworthy in the context of Nebraska's legal history, particularly given that before Richards' execution, the state had recorded only one other execution, in 1863, a mere four years before it became part of the United States.

These events, spanning from 1853 to 1871, unfolded during a transformative period in Nebraska's history. They occurred against the backdrop of a developing criminal law and justice system, reflecting the challenges and complexities of governing a rapidly changing society.

Stephen D. Richards' life was a tapestry of dramatic shifts and dark turns, beginning in Wheeling, Virginia, where he was born on March 18, 1856. Growing up in a family with five sisters and a brother, Richards' early life was marked by frequent relocations, from Monroe County to Noble County in Ohio, and eventually to the Quaker village of Mount Pleasant. His mother, a devout Methodist, and his father, a farmer with no particular religious inclinations, provided a contrasting backdrop to his upbringing.

Richards' school days in Mount Pleasant were uneventful yet significant. Described as well-behaved by his teachers, he adhered to his mother's wishes by regularly attending Sunday school and church. However, life took a pivotal turn when Richards' mother passed away on September 16, 1871, an event that would precede a series of radical changes in his life.

As Richards stepped into adulthood, his life seemed to veer off its predictable course. At twenty, he became engaged to Anna Millhorne and found himself mingling with individuals of dubious character. This was the beginning of his foray into the world of counterfeit bills, a path that led him away from Mount Pleasant in pursuit of greater ambitions.

Richards' journey took him through Iowa, where he worked on farms and, in a grim twist, served as an attendant at the Iowa Lunatic Asylum in Mount Pleasant, Iowa. His role there, burying deceased patients, profoundly impacted his view of humanity, turning him callous to the point of seeing people as nothing more than 'meat'. This chilling perspective was reported by The New York Times as a transformative phase in Richards' life.

Leaving the asylum in October 1876, Richards began a nomadic existence across the Midwest, dabbling in various jobs and occasionally associating with train robbers. His travels took him through Kansas City and Nebraska, where he claimed involvement in several gunfights, adopting a cavalier attitude towards human life. During this time, he assumed various aliases, including William Hudson, shedding and adopting identities as easily as changing locations.

Stephen D. Richards' confession following his final arrest paints a chilling picture of his exploits in Nebraska and Iowa during 1876 and 1877, revealing a trail marked by violence and cold-blooded killings. In this dark narrative, he admitted to ending the lives of four men, with his first act of murder occurring shortly after his arrival in Kearney in late 1876.

The tale begins with an encounter that quickly spiraled into violence. While traversing the Nebraska countryside on horseback, Richards came across a stranger. The two decided to camp near Dobytown, although some newspapers later reported the location as near Sand Hills. As night fell, a card game ensued, with Richards claiming victory over most of the stranger's money. The next morning, as they headed towards Kearney, the game's loser demanded his money back. Richards' refusal led to a confrontation where, in a fit of rage, he fatally shot the man above the left eye and disposed of his body in the Platte River.

But the saga didn't end there. Days later, Richards met another man, this time near Walker's Ranch. The stranger, having seen Richards with his earlier victim, began inquiring about his whereabouts. As the conversation unfolded, Richards realized that this man was not just a curious passerby but the business partner and friend of the man he had killed. Feeling cornered and fearing exposure, Richards made a fateful decision to eliminate this potential threat. In a cold and calculated move, he shot the man in the back of the head and disposed of his body, later selling the man's horse in a nearby town.

As Richards continued his journey, he stopped at the home of Jasper Harlson, a rumored train robber. There, he encountered Jasper's wife, Mary, a woman described as a "free talker." Noticing bloodstains on Richards' shirt, she commented on them, to which Richards casually joked that they must have come from the men he had murdered, abruptly ending the conversation.

Stephen D. Richards' journey into a world of crime and violence continued in Cedar Rapids, Iowa, where he deftly used counterfeit money to purchase a horse and buggy. But when the seller realized the bills were fake and confronted Richards, demanding either real money or the return of his property, Richards' response was as cold as it was final: he shot the man dead and hastily buried the body, disappearing into the shadows once more.

In March 1877, Richards' path crossed with a young man named Gemge in Grand Island, Nebraska. Together, they embarked on horseback towards Kearney. Their journey, however, was marred by a deadly altercation. One night, camped between Lowell and Kearney along the Platte River, Richards awoke Gemge at 3:00 a.m., claiming it was time to depart. Infuriated at being woken up prematurely, Gemge hurled insults at Richards, escalating the dispute to a point of no return. Richards, feeling threatened by Gemge's aggressive stance and the brandishing of a revolver, made a split-second decision. Drawing his own weapon, he shot Gemge in the head, abruptly ending their argument and partnership.

Richards' nomadic life soon led him to Kearney, where he checked into a local hotel under the alias F.A. Hoge. It was there he reconnected with familiar faces: George "Dutch Henry" Johnson, Hurst, and a man known as Mr.

Burns. But this reunion was short-lived. On March 21, Richards and Burns found themselves under arrest. Initially unaware of the specific accusations, Richards suspected it was related to Gemge's murder. However, they were actually being held under suspicion for the murder of a man named Peter Geteway. Richards maintained his innocence regarding Geteway's death, and though he was quickly acquitted, Burns' fate hung in the balance due to an accusation from a "sporting lady" he knew. Ultimately, Burns too was acquitted for lack of evidence linking him to the crime.

In the simmering heat of June 1878, in the dusty town of Kearney, Richards found himself behind bars, accused of larceny—a charge he vehemently denied. Amidst the clanging of jail bars, a chance reunion occurred with Mary L. Harlson, a woman entangled in her own web of suspicion for allegedly aiding in a daring jailbreak.

Their paths crossed in the most unlikely of places, leading to a clandestine agreement: six months hence, Mary would sell her property to Richards for $600. Once free, Richards roamed the expanse of Nebraska, conducting business in Hastings, Bloomington, and Grand Island, before arriving at the Harlson homestead in Kearney County on October 18, 1878. There, a transaction took place—Mary transferred her property to Richards, who lingered at the homestead for weeks.

The New York Daily Herald later spun a narrative of deceit and ulterior motives, alleging that Richards and Harlson's marriage on November 2 was nothing but a ruse—a ploy to gain control of Harlson's land. However, a dark plot was simmering beneath this veneer of domesticity. Richards harbored a chilling secret, one that he feared Mary's loquacious nature might expose. To protect his past and silence her forever, he resolved to commit an unthinkable act.

In the pre-dawn hours of November 3, 1878, while another man named Brown attended to the farm, Richards, armed with a spade and a sinister plan, carried out a horrific deed. The household awoke not to the promise of a new day, but to the horror of Richards' axe. The chilling details vary—some accounts speak of a smoothing iron used in the gruesome act, others of a brutal assault. Richards himself claimed it was done swiftly, in their sleep. Yet, the aftermath was undeniable: a bloodied floor, the lifeless bodies of Mary and her three children—Daisy, Mabel, and little Jasper, cruelly nicknamed "Jesse"—and a man who sat down to breakfast with the calmness of the abyss.

As the sun rose, Richards buried the evidence of his crime in a hastily dug grave. When inquiries about the Harlsons arose, his response was calculated and cold: they had left with Brown, whereabouts unknown. It wasn't until December 11 that the grim truth emerged, revealing the final resting place of the Harlsons, concealed under a haystack rather than buried, contradicting Richards' later claims.

On a cold December day in 1878, a sinister plot unfolded in the quiet countryside. Richards, a man shrouded in mystery and known to some as "Dick Richardson," entered into a seemingly innocent agreement with his neighbor, a 26-year-old Swedish immigrant named Peter Anderson. Richards offered to assist Anderson with work on his property, a gesture that would soon reveal its dark undertones.

The day took a chilling turn when Anderson fell violently ill after consuming a meal prepared by Richards. Suspecting foul play, Anderson confided in a neighbor his fears of being poisoned. The tension escalated rapidly, culminating in a confrontation the following day that would seal both men's fates.

In a brutal and violent clash, Richards and Anderson fought fiercely. The details of Anderson's demise are mired in mystery and contradiction. Some say he was ruthlessly beaten to death with a hammer or hatchet, others whisper of a gunshot echoing through the air. The only certainty was the grim discovery that followed: Anderson's lifeless body, hidden beneath a pile of coal in the cellar of his own house.

Richards vehemently denied the accusations of poisoning, claiming such methods were beneath him. He portrayed the deadly encounter as an act of self-defense, insisting that it was Anderson who had brandished a knife. Despite his assertions, the community was left to grapple with the shocking reality of the violence that had erupted amidst them.

In the aftermath, Anderson was laid to rest in the quiet solace of Bethany Cemetery in Axtell, Nebraska. His tragic end, at the hands of a man he had trusted, became a somber reminder of the lurking dangers in the rural landscape, where secrets and betrayals could have deadly consequences.

In a desperate bid to evade the consequences of his heinous acts, Richards hastily decided to abandon Kearney, anticipating the imminent discovery of his gruesome deeds. Under the cloak of evening, he was feverishly hitching up Anderson's horses for his escape when fate intervened. Anderson's concerned neighbors, puzzled by his mysterious disappearance, arrived and confronted Richards. Offering a deceptive assurance that Anderson was inside, Richards seized this moment of distraction to make a daring escape on horseback, setting off towards Bloomington.

Richards' flight from justice was marked by urgency and cunning. He traversed the land by various means—horse, train, and on foot—making his way through Omaha and Chicago. During this frenetic journey, he joined forces with Jasper Harlson and another fugitive, weaving a path through Wheeling, West Virginia, and into Ohio. Their journey led them to Mount Pleasant, Richards' childhood home, a place where his past and present collided.

Meanwhile, Nebraska Governor Silas Garber, determined to bring Richards to justice, issued an arrest warrant on December 16, 1878, with a $200 bounty for his capture. But Richards, undeterred by the looming threat, audaciously attended a ballroom dance in Mount Pleasant on December 20, accompanied by two mysterious women. His brazen presence did not go unnoticed. The town was abuzz with whispers and wanted posters bearing his likeness, and Constable McGrew, with the help of a penitentiary guard, recognized Richards.

Armed with shotguns, the lawmen approached Richards in a field outside the town. Surprisingly, Richards, usually so quick to violence, was unarmed and opted for surrender. He later claimed that he had been ready to fight, but the presence of the women swayed his decision. He chillingly remarked that had he been alone, McGrew would likely have been a dead man, as he would have resorted to gunfire.

Richards speculated that if he had evaded capture, he would have returned to Nebraska, ironically considering it the least likely place for anyone to search for him. His twisted logic and daring escapes painted the portrait of a man constantly dancing on the edge of danger, always one step ahead, yet inevitably ensnared by his own audacious actions.

The tale of Richards' arrest is shrouded in a patchwork of conflicting reports, each adding layers of intrigue to his already enigmatic story. The Wheeling Daily Intelligencer spun a version where Richards, upon his arrival near Mount Pleasant, was recognized and detained by a former acquaintance, assisted by another individual. In a twist, another account places his capture in early 1879 in Austin, Texas. Adding to the mystery, a modern narrative credits Pinkerton agents with identifying and apprehending the elusive Richards, known in this telling as Samuel Richards.

Even Richards' physical description became a subject of debate. Newspapers painted him as a towering figure, over six feet tall, with a robust build, dark hair, and piercing blue eyes. This image, however, clashed with the observations of Dr. Moreland, who conducted a phrenological examination prior to Richards' execution. Dr. Moreland noted Richards as having light brown hair and dark gray eyes, a description further muddled by a spectator at Richards' execution, who recalled his eyes as steel grey, almost bluish, and his hair as dark brown.

Amidst these varying accounts, The Workingman's Friend, a Leavenworth, Kansas newspaper, reported that Chicago authorities received a portion of the reward for Richards' capture, suggesting a network of law enforcement was involved in his eventual downfall.

After his arrest, Richards found himself behind bars in Steubenville, Ohio. It was here that he penned two articles for the local newspaper, shockingly confessing to nine murders over three years. The task of extraditing Richards fell to Sheriff David Anderson of Buffalo County, Nebraska, and Sheriff Martin of Kearney County. They were acutely aware of the public's outrage and feared a lynching if Richards were brought back to the scenes of his crimes. Thus, a decision was made to initially avoid these localities.

At the time of his arrest, there was speculation that Richards might have been part of, or even the leader of, a notorious gang of outlaws. Law enforcement linked him to the nine murders he confessed to and entertained the possibility of more. This speculation was met with skepticism by The Nebraska State Journal.

As his trial loomed, Richards grimly predicted his own conviction and hanging. He was moved to a jail in Omaha and then transferred to Kearney by train. His arrival in Kearney was met with a seething crowd, a tangible manifestation of the townsfolk's rage. Authorities, wary of the threat of lynching, took extra precautions for Richards' safety. During his transfer to the depot, Richards seemed almost taken aback by the sheer size of the crowd, quipping about the entire town turning out to see him. Despite the palpable tension, the crowd eventually dispersed, and Richards' stay in Kearney passed without further incident.

In the quiet town of Minden, Nebraska, the trial of Richards commenced on January 16, 1879, under the watchful eye of Judge William Gaslin. The courtroom, charged with anticipation, witnessed a legal battle between the prosecution, helmed by District Attorney Scofield, and Richards' defense, led by a lawyer named Savage. The charges were grave: two indictments for first-degree murder, encompassing the brutal slaying of the Harlson family and Anderson.

Richards, cloaked in a guise of innocence, pled not guilty. He staunchly defended his actions, claiming the killing of Anderson was a desperate act of self-defense. The prosecution's strategy unfolded with precision, calling seven witnesses who painted a vivid picture of the grim scene where Anderson was discovered.

The climax of the trial arrived when Richards took the stand. Under Scofield's probing questions, he confessed to killing Anderson with a hammer amidst a fiery argument but maintained the stance of self-defense, alleging that Anderson had menacingly reached for a hatchet. The prosecution delivered a damning blow by presenting the very hammer used in the murder, which Richards chillingly confirmed as the weapon.

After a mere two hours of contemplation, the jury delivered their verdict: guilty on all counts. Richards was condemned to the gallows, his execution scheduled for April 26, 1879. Throughout the proceedings and upon hearing his fate, Richards displayed a demeanor described as "cheerful and indifferent," a chilling contrast to the gravity of his crimes.

A twist emerged in the aftermath of his conviction, reported only by the Sedalia Weekly Bazoo. Richards, in a desperate turn, had allegedly smuggled a knife into his cell, intending to end his own life. However, before he could enact his plan, the authorities intervened, seizing the weapon. This startling detail, however, stands alone, uncorroborated by other newspaper accounts, adding yet another layer of mystery to the enigmatic figure of Richards.

As Richards was escorted back to Nebraska, his demeanor, as reported by the Omaha Herald, was one of chilling nonchalance. He displayed an unsettling indifference to his fate, remarking he was as ready to face death in Kearney

Junction as anywhere else. This unnerving calm set the stage for what would become one of the most dramatic and chaotic executions in Nebraska's history.

Sheriff Martin, foreseeing the public's morbid curiosity, declared Richards' execution in Minden an open event, despite his apprehension about the potential for a violent, unruly crowd. In a controversial move, an enclosure was built around the gallows, and tickets granting access to this restricted area were sold. Richards, in a peculiar twist, extended invitations to members of the press he had befriended during his imprisonment. This ticket to history is now a preserved artifact in the collection of the Nebraska Historical Society.

On the day of execution, estimates of the crowd's size ranged wildly, from 2,000 to a staggering 25,000. The atmosphere was electric, teetering on the brink of chaos. As the crowd surged against the barriers, guards struggled to maintain order. Rolf Johnson, a witness to the pandemonium, described a surreal tug of war between the guards and the mob, who ultimately triumphed in tearing down the enclosure and spilling onto the prairie.

At precisely 1:00 p.m., the arrival of Richards, escorted by Martin and his deputy, momentarily quelled the crowd. Richards, standing on the gallows, launched into a fervent speech, maintaining his innocence in the Harlson murders and reasserting his claim of self-defense in Anderson's death. He proclaimed his newfound religious faith, leading the crowd in a hymn, and his final words, imploring Jesus to be with him, echoed in the charged air.

The execution, carried out at 1:17 p.m., was a protracted affair, with reports claiming it took fifteen minutes for Richards to die. His death marked a grim milestone as the first execution in Nebraska's history since its incorporation into the United States.

In the aftermath, the macabre fascination with Richards continued. Local doctors, eager to perform an autopsy, were rebuffed by Richards before his execution. Despite being buried in Minden, his body was not left to rest in peace. It was stolen, returned, and then desecrated again, with his bones callously scattered on the streets of Kearney. In a bizarre final chapter, Richards' skull found its way into the Kearney County Gazette's office window, displayed for all to see. The fate of his skull remains a mystery, its whereabouts and status lost to time.

Conclusion

As the shadows of history's most infamous axe murders are explored, it becomes evident that these chilling tales reveal much about human nature, justice, and the fine line between normalcy and brutality. These stories, from the infamous Lizzie Borden case to the lesser-known but equally harrowing Hinterkaifeck murders in Germany, are not mere sensational tales; they are profound insights into the darker aspects of the human psyche and societal norms.

The timelessness of these crimes is striking. Regardless of the era or location, they evoke a universal shock and disbelief, challenging the perception of a civilized society being far removed from its barbaric past. The axe, a primitive yet effective weapon, symbolizes this brutal rupture of societal norms.

The psychology of the perpetrators remains a topic of intense fascination. These individuals, driven by a complex interplay of psychological issues, personal vendettas, societal pressures, or sometimes an inexplicable lack of motive, reflect the multifaceted nature of human behavior and its darkest potentials.

In the communities affected by these crimes, an undercurrent of fear and suspicion often lingered, particularly in cases that remained unsolved, like the Villisca axe murders. These unsolved mysteries underscored the fragility of trust within communities, revealing how easily it can be shattered by violence and fear.

The stories of history's notorious axe murders are not just macabre curiosities; they are cautionary tales reflecting the complexities of human nature and societal structures. They challenge the understanding of the fine line between sanity and madness, justice and injustice, and the quest to comprehend the human soul's unfathomable depths.

Perhaps the most unsettling aspect of these stories is the reminder that beneath the veneer of civilization lie the primal, the unexplained, and the incomprehensible, as capable of surfacing today as in the past. The echoes of these axe murders are not merely echoes from a distant past but a continuous whisper in the collective consciousness, a reminder of the need to remember, reflect, and remain vigilant in the face of such timeless and profound mysteries.

Bibliography

Anon. "Life and Confession of Stephen Dee Richards: The Murderer of Nine Persons, Executed at Minden, Nebraska, April 26, 1879". State Journal Co, 1 May 1879.

Bartle, Ronald. "Lizzie Borden and the Massachusetts Axe Murders". Waterside Press, Sherfield-on-Loddon, Hampshire, 2017.

Bastoni, Mark. "Isles of Shoals Murders | Horror on Smuttynose Island". New England, 9 March 2022, https://newengland.com/yankee/history/smutt ynose-murders/.

Brown, Arnold. "Lizzie Borden: The Legend, the Truth, the Final Chapter". Rutledge Hill Press, Nashville, Tennessee, 1991.

Bunney, Kathy. "The Ship of Seven Murders: A True Story of Madness & Murder". Collins Press, 2011.

Conliffe, Ciararn. "John Lynch, The Berrima Axe Murderer". Headstuff, 3 July 2016, https://headstuff.org/culture/history/john-lynch-the-berrima-ax e-murderer/.

Davis, Miriam C. "The Axeman of New Orleans". Chicago Review Press Incorporated, 2017.

Estep, Richard. "A Nightmare in Villisca: Investigating the Haunted Axe Murder House". Word Wise, 2020.

Gauthreaux, Alan. "Dark Bayou: Infamous Louisiana Homicides". Mcfarland & Co, 2015.

Golla, Guido. "Hinterkaifeck: Autopsie eines Sechsfachmordes". Norderstedt, 2016.

Host, Your Intrepid. "Why History is Horrifying: Massacre on the High Seas". Why I Love Horror, 18 November 2022, https://whyhorror.blog/2022/1 1/18/why-mary-russell/.

James, Bill, and Rachel McCarthy James. "The Man from the Train: The Solving of a Century-Old Serial Killer Mystery". Simon and Schuster, 19 September 2017.

Katz, Hélèna. "Cold Cases: Famous Unsolved Mysteries, Crimes, and Disappearances in America". ABC-CLIO, Santa Barbara, CA, 2010.

Kirkbride, Wayne. "Dmz: A Story of the Panmunjom Axe Murder". Hollym Intl Corp, 1984.

O'Connor, Jessica. "The Story Of Christopher Porco, The College Student Who Brutally Attacked His Parents With An Ax". All That's Interesting, 20 September 2022, https://allthatsinteresting.com/christopher-porco.

Robinson, J Dennis. "Mystery on the Isles of Shoals: Closing the Case on the Smuttynose Ax Murders of 1873". Skyhorse, 2014.

Rockefeller, J. D. "America's 14 Worst Serial Killers". J.D. Rockefeller, 2016.

Shipton, Julia. "Stephen Dee Richards: The 'Nebraska Fiend'". Murder Murder News, 25 March, https://murdermurder.news/news/stephen-dee-richards.

Smyth, Jonathan. "The Notorious Axe Murderer of Berrima". The Anglo-Celt, 18 April 2021, https://www.anglocelt.ie/2021/04/18/the-notorious-axe-murderer-of-berrima/.